R.O.Blechman

Behind the Lines

R.O.Blechman

Behind the Lines

Foreword by
Maurice Sendak

Art Direction by
Bea Feitler

Hudson Hills Press, New York

First Edition
© 1980 by R. O. Blechman
All rights reserved under International and Pan-American
Copyright Conventions
Published in the United States by Hudson Hills Press, Inc.,
Suite 4323, 30 Rockefeller Plaza, New York, N.Y. 10112
Trade distribution by Simon & Schuster, a division of Gulf &
Western Corporation, New York

———————

Library of Congress Cataloging in Publication Data
Blechman, R. O.
R. O. Blechman, behind the lines.
1. Blechman, R. O.   2. Artists—
United States—Biography.   I. Title.
N6537.B563A2   741.6'092'4 [B]   80-15191
ISBN 0-933920-07-5

———————

EDITOR AND PUBLISHER: PAUL ANBINDER
COPY-EDITOR: JULIANA WU
DESIGNER: CARL BARILE
PRODUCTION: BILL KOBASZ
COMPOSITION: KORDON TYPOGRAPHERS, INC.
Manufactured in Japan by Dai Nippon Printing Company

Contents

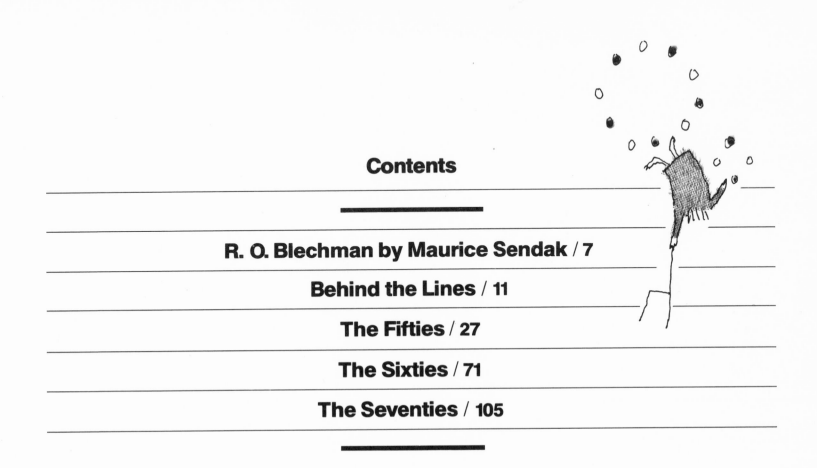

R. O. Blechman

I was introduced to R. O. Blechman in 1952, in the then center of my universe, the Eighth Street Bookshop in Greenwich Village. It was not the flesh-and-blood Blechman—I had little hope then of knowing the man—but his spirit, voice, and immensely rich talent all manifest in a slender volume called *The Juggler of Our Lady*. It was a fine moment. I was twenty-four years old, just recently escaped from that dread *shtetl* called Brooklyn and nursing a new career in a now-vanished, inexpensive Big Apple.

Much to the distress of my parents, I had firmly turned my back on any formal art training and wanted only to earn my own living in New York City. I had already illustrated three or four books and my method of looking at, and learning and stealing from, nineteenth-century illustrators (and those few contemporaries who suited my purpose) only confirmed a stubbornly ingrained instinct: self-reliance at all costs. And it cost. I am convinced that the surface quality of my work matured slowly because of this inner recoil from formal training. It was not a proud choice; rather, that is how I was, temperamentally and psychically—forever tuned out of school.

I treasure my first edition *Juggler*, and the memory of its effect on me is still fresh. I assumed, of course, that this Blechman was a wise and ancient sage; the book was rich in graphic and psychological detail, and I was busy looking for creative gurus. I've never quite recovered from the fact that Bob is younger than I am (he was born in 1930). The silliness of this detail can best be explained, perhaps, by my own 1952 consciousness of immaturity and the genuine need for a teacher outside the schoolroom.

The *Juggler*, delicate and modest though he was, powerfully pulled together in a single work a variety of disparate elements, which, up to that point in my career, I had imagined unjoinable. I have a very selective memory—in short, almost no memory at all, except for what passionately and selfishly serves my creative purpose. But, though *The Juggler* lies here at hand for me to refer to, I can remember that Eighth Street Bookshop Day, a day in ancient history when one could stand and read an entire book in a bookstore without surly gibes from the salesclerks. Perhaps it's wrong to linger so long over Blechman's *Juggler*; after all, it was only the beginning of a complex body of work that, astoundingly, grew constantly more subtle and refined without ever losing its secure hold on real feeling and, even more critical, its child's vision. Yet *The Juggler* is surely the ground plan for everything that came after. Simply, Blechman was Blechman in 1952 and, though pieces such as *The Emperor's New Armor* and other choice works are superior in sophistication of style and view, *The Juggler*, in a real sense, pretty much said it all. It may be a commonplace, but there is no underestimating the pleasure to be derived from staring back over a long career and sympathetically eyeing the first work that fumblingly—even hastily—set out all the themes of one's lifetime, as if for a sumptuous but too ample dinner. My own first "grand plan" book was unabashedly if endearingly fumbling, but Blechman's was not. Now that I know Bob, I have no doubt that the entire book was tirelessly done over and over until, finally, it squeaked past the artist's harsh approval.

Only a week ago, when I visited Bob's studio for the purpose of collecting a mass of Blechmaniana for this introduction, I asked him for a copy of *The Juggler* to peruse. (I did not want to flip through my personal copy, and Bob is a sufficient book nut to understand such finickyness.) He promptly presented me with a first edition—autographed to Ronald Searle. I was a little taken aback until he explained in his quiet, serious way that he had never presented this copy to Searle because he'd been dissatisfied with the *look* of his finely handwritten salutation on the flyleaf. I was not so much surprised as stunned by what that simple explanation implied. After all, the entire *Juggler* is in Bob's very particular calligraphy, and I could only vaguely imagine how many times he'd done *it* over.

That thought brings me back again to 1952 on Eighth Street between Fifth and Sixth Avenues. The book was (and still is) bound in a dusky gray-blue paper over boards, and wonderfully, perfectly, the spine (and a bit more on either side) are in gold. I am frankly "fetishistic" about beautiful books and always have been. Some of my earliest, happiest experiences centered on the look, feel, and smell of books; reading was the least part of this sensual ritual. It was easy, then, for Blechman's binding to have promptly snared me; but what effectively sprung the trap was (and remember, I was seeing him for the very first time) Blechman's peculiar, sprawling calligraphy on the spine of his book. What did this modest, crooked, and seemingly "unprofessional" hand lettering have to do with the sophistication of dusky blue and gold? Everything. Cantalbert, our juggler, is, so to speak, already there on the spine and binding; the aesthetic essence of the work has quietly been stated. It is the perfect, brief overture to what is about to come. Such a gentle, abstract comment on the book's interior purpose is no easy business. But then, Blechman is no easy artist. As for my rhapsodizing over the exquisite variations in lettering on the title and copyright pages (there is a fierceness to the all-rights-reserved line compared to the trusting, open-eyed copyright line, and *that* juxtaposed with the charming certainty of his "a sort-of-Christmas story"); if it sounds like too much precious conceit on my part—too bad! It's all there—suggesting so much—and we've not even begun the actual story! But I'll leave out the saga of the juggler—much has been written about him: he has won prestigious awards and been twice filmed. Besides, one purpose of the present volume—a work, in my opinion, long overdue—is to recreate this famous first book. If the reader is a genuine fetishist, then it will be his or her happy fate to seek out a first edition (it won't be easy to find—just great fun).

What multiple messages did the good *Juggler* pass on to this eager young artist? One could neatly list some of the more obvious: It offered hope that one day I too might have autonomous control of a published work; that every detail, so crucial to the whole, could be rendered by the artist. It also encouraged the latent wish to write one's own book and thus create—through story, pictures, type, layout, binding, choice of paper (and weight of paper), and overall design—a firm, personal statement. It suggested that elements, so intriguing and once considered contradictory, could be, with ingenuity, combined.

The comic strip, animated cartoon, and silent-movie comedy are all lovingly part of Blechman's background and style. For me, they were my nursery school of art. Mickey Mouse, Little Nemo, Krazy Kat, Charlie Chaplin, and Buster Keaton were the original sources, the wellsprings of excitement and creative stimulation. But they were, for me then, isolated forms navigating through my imagination like so many circling moons. *The Juggler*, in one giant step, pulled them together. The mix is so subtle, so understated, it might easily be overlooked. I was too eager and sniffing to miss the point. Here was a book that, with a magician's cool grace, brought it all off. The sheer surface look of it intrigued me. I was not to know then—or even imagine—how Blechman would wring every graphic ounce out of his wriggly style. It is, at first glance, a dangerous style for an artist to lock into. It's so specific, so special; where can you go from there? Blechman's refinement of that style—the paradox of his further condensing his miniature hieroglyphs to draw larger meanings—is a marvel.

It all has to do with the man, of course. Blechman never took himself or his work too seriously. His "*mensch*-ness" expanded as he aged and the searching, stuttering line grew with him, though it seemed on paper to have nearly blown away. It became essence—

the merest tool. His many imitators—the mass of counterfeit Blechmans who do indeed prove the folly of the entrapping style—are prisoners of style, helplessly bound to repeat themselves ad nauseam. Style, however, became Blechman's handmaiden and, rather than freezing into a permanent jitter, the Blechman look has a gorgeous fluidity. Every nuance and comic (or tragic) suggestion seems barely breathed on a page. His qualities of taste, intelligence, and—most vital—his instinct never to stray into forms that will betray him have allowed Blechman to express himself in a variety of ways that have enhanced the quality of American life.

A Blechman ad makes its point beautifully—and quietly. As a worker in this form he is part of a small cadre of gifted artists who have raised the level of advertising art. This, I am aware, is a banality (the pages of the scrumptious *Graphis* magazine are, after all, devoted to such artists, and Blechman has been well served by a number of illustrated articles). Even here, I would insist, Blechman has made a special mark. There is something devilishly delightful in the contradiction of blank, bold Irving Trust logo (there is no suggestion of humor) and the familiar Blechman wriggle making a witty jest of a day at the bank. The fatuous bank clerk (we know he is fatuous) asking his customer how in the world he ever got his parrot to talk, the parrot turns and answers, "I just keep repeating words to him." And we notice for the first time the look of total imbecility on the customer's face, and the bank clerk's priceless expression. How, in God's name, *did* Blechman give him that look of embarrassed dismay when hardly a line has moved? The Sony ads, perked up with remarkable bits of fresh Blechmanish color, are favorites of mine; for example, the violinist who unceremoniously dumps his priceless instrument and rapturously tucks a Sony tape deck under his chin and stands, bow hanging limply from left hand, listening and watching the Full Color Sound of Sony. Blechman's color, by the by, is so sparingly used that it never ceases to astonish. Like everything else Blechman, it is a very personal palette. Sony should indeed sound so good!

Bob has made his points in the pages of the *New York Times Book Review,* on the covers of the *New Yorker,* and in too many other places to catalog here. It is difficult to resist the temptation to point out personal favorites, such as the *National Lampoon* piece called "The Runaway." Look it up in the pages of this book and mark well the expressions on the poor dog's face. The sadness and comedy of the piece are quintessential Blechman. Then check out the superb *New Yorker* cover with Bob's cock-eyed vision of a contemporary—if somewhat pompous—New York skyline sporting charming but quite unworkable windmills. Is it only because I so dislike the World Trade Center towers that I see the windmills as judgmental x's crossing architectural errors out of existence? (The lovely Empire State discreetly hides her x's behind.) Is Blechman good-naturedly humbling all those haughty and slightly ridiculous Grand Dames—or is it just his whimsical, wry reminder of our humble past? It doesn't matter. And last, his superb *black* black-panther picture for the *New York Times Book Review* and his other happy silhouette spoof of the Howard Johnson logo on the same pages.

Although I admire most of Blechman's graphic excursions, my heart, admittedly, is and always has been with him in the realm of books. And almost my favorite Blechman item—though not precisely a book—is his pamphlet entitled *The Emperor's New Armor*, a rather fierce takeoff on Hans Christian Andersen's famous fairy tale. I will leave the plot to the reader (except to say that the king's final words are so funny and so dreadful that they chink, perhaps more than anything he's written, the armor of one R. O. Blechman), and rhapsodize again on the harmonious whole of this simple four-page pamphlet. It is printed on ordinary (cheap, actually) yellowing paper, but the king's armor is luxurious, colored (it looks as if by hand) in silver. The combination is ingenious, perfect and pure best Blechman.

I have very consciously stayed away from any analysis of Bob's work—any groping with those much-mentioned themes, or coming out with a coherent "this is what Blechman is saying." That would be ludicrous, surely. Nor do I like putting his work (as some have) in large, suitable categories such as Fragile Man Against Unfeeling World. But there is one aspect of Blechman's art that touches me personally and is something of an obsession; I would even suggest it is the unconscious bond that ties us together as artists. It is something I fleetingly mentioned earlier on: Blechman's child view. *Child view* is often translated into *creative view,* but they are not the same thing. There is a fierce, first freshness implied in the former that is part of an elaborate sensibility in the latter. This matter seriously concerns me because, as an artist doing books for children, I depend almost entirely on an uninhibited intercourse with this primitive, uncensored self.

A beautiful passage by Roger Shattuck, writing about the composer Erik Satie, comes to mind:

The more one learns about Satie, the more one comes to see him as a man who performed every contortion in order to keep sight of his childhood. Like a child who twists his body as he walks in order not to lose sight of his shadow, Satie made sure that the most treasured part of his past was always at his side.

I personally can attest to the ordeal of maintaining the child vision in adult life, and I suspect Bob Blechman has suffered the same dual perception. But it is this very quality that informs his work and accounts for its unique appeal.

Bob and I are typical colleagues/friends—we hardly ever see each other. This is more my fault. His exquisite wife, Moisha, has often asked me to visit. I've never even seen the Blechman children. This doesn't, I hope, make me less a Blechman friend. It only points up that infernal, interior insistence on work that imperiously contradicts one's normal, gregarious inclinations. The Blechmans understand this. My best friends in the profession are people I rarely see but whose natures and work I love. I have no recollection of how Bob and I met—when or where—or the number of times we've seen each other. We are, nonetheless, solid friends, and that feels good.

When Blechman approached me to be part of his "Simple Gifts" TV special, I accepted despite my previous, harrowing TV experience. I did so because I completely trusted my friend. I knew he would attend to detail with the same maniacal obsessiveness as I would myself. It turned out that I could not be involved as much as I wanted, but when I was, I had the great satisfaction of seeing my work in the hands of dedicated professionals. It seemed to go without a hitch. Of course, that is nonsense—it was anything but smooth sailing. It is this self-effacing smoothness that belies a Blechman project, that comforts the artist and hides from his anxious eyes all the scraping and rubbing and punching that go into the concocting of a TV special. People working closely with Blechman will perhaps mutter at his stiff-necked perfectionism, but everyone respects it. And if I am known in my profession as something of a large pain when it comes to the manufacture of my books, Blechman is rightly nothing less when it comes to something that bears his name. I had the keenest pleasure in watching my little Christmas overture to "Simple Gifts," and with that went the astonishing—for me—security and trust in my colleague's high standards. I had worried, but the finished product was proof of my initial, eminently well-placed confidence. That confidence—and affection—marks the quality of our friendship. We expect the best from each other. Blechman's imperfection—being two years my junior—I have long since forgiven.

MAURICE SENDAK
Ridgefield, Connecticut
February 17, 1980

I was born when zeppelins were still flying over Brooklyn. They would turn slowly over Avenue M and make their final approach to Lakewood, New Jersey. To a young boy, they were part of the natural order of things. Zeppelins belonged to a world where Fred Astaire danced the Continental and Douglas Fairbanks swung in arcs as wide as the double-thick cuffs of my father's pants and the silver-fox scarf flung over my mother's shoulder. A zeppelin represented time and space to spare, and to a boy growing up in the Thirties the immense shadow it cast was reassuring.

Sometimes I wondered what the passengers saw as they looked down on Flatbush. They could not have lingered long. After the Manhattan skyline, we must have been a disappointment: a gray patch between the vivid, blue ocean and the green of New Jersey, a dull passage between bright entrances and exits.

What they might have seen, I learned when I was seven years old. One day my Uncle Nat, an amateur pilot, took me up in his biplane. As we flew over Flatbush, he turned to me—hunched beside him in the open cockpit, my eyes well below the edge—and shouted, "HOME!" He pointed below, dipping the wings of the plane for emphasis. "Home?" I looked. There, somewhere below me, among the hundreds of tiny squares, were my mother and father . . . my nurse, Grace . . . Grandma . . . ! I burst into tears. The sobs must have pierced the engine's roar. Uncle Nat straightened the plane, turned it around, and returned to the airport. He never took me flying again.

Uncle Nat was not only an amateur pilot, he was also an amateur cartoonist. When he visited my family, his after-dinner drawings were eagerly traded by my brother and me. But we both knew that Uncle Nat was not a real artist. That distinction belonged to his sister, Aunt Kitty. She painted in oil, the only serious medium. Her output was restricted to bunches of flowers, exuberant and vivid as her blond hair and the knobby colored-glass objects she collected, which glowed as the Flatbush sun burst through them, continuing the bright paths of irises outside her stucco home.

I did not draw as a child, except for the strips I made for my home movies. My theater was a shoe box with a rectangle cut out for the screen. I used two pegs to move the long strips of paper that were my picture stories: Frank Buck catching wild animals alive; Wimpy devouring dozens of hamburgers; the Polish cavalry invading Berlin and Nazi Germany capitulating. Virtue triumphed; it had to, because I desperately needed the escape happy endings provided.

My mother was a beautiful woman who was very young, and looked even younger than her years. Mr. Cohen, the grocer, said she couldn't be my mother at all, but had to be my older sister. How proud I was to have a mother so much admired by him! But it was at home, seated at the polished grand piano, that my love and pride were greatest. Wearing a pink moiré gown, my mother swayed to the rhythms of "Begin the Beguine," "Tea for Two," and "Deep Purple." "When the deep purple falls over sleepy garden walls," she would close her eyes and sing, only slightly thinner than the lush piano accompaniment that shifted easily from key to key, like the purple dripping and flowing from garden wall to garden wall. "Yes," I thought, as she moved on to "Did You Ever See a Dream Walking?," "Yes, I have," although I was not at all sure how a Dream could be Walking. What I *was* sure of, however, was that *I* was seated next to my mother, and that Mr. Cohen, my father, and my brother were not.

But this Dream could, like the sweetest dew from heaven, vanish in the harsh air of day. My mother sometimes, suddenly, inexplicably, would turn on me, and her beloved son would become a worm in the family apple, a thorn in her moiré side. "You made your bed," I would hear, "now lie in it!" No Hindu's bed of nails could be more painful than this bed I was accused of making. I would cry for solace to my nurse, Grace, or to my grandmother.

Grandma
Blechman at home.

My father in
the country, 1920.

My mother
and Aunt Kitty.

And always, enveloped in their ample arms, the solace came, the pain passed.

As I became older, the shifts between heaven and hell grew more frequent, more unpredictable, the limbos between them increasingly shorter. The Dream walked less and less. More often than not, the Dream sat silently at the piano, lips pursed, eyes open and inward-looking.

My father, at least, had the virtue of consistency. He was cold and distant, like an Arrow Collar illustration. My brother and I competed for the love my father rarely could give and my mother could give only fitfully. My brother's competitiveness sometimes took a violent form. *Slap,* he struck my shoulder at the beach, *slap,* on the shoulder again, *slap,* in the same place, although at this point his target was in full motion. "Cancer," he would say, *slap,* "is caused by repeated blows, did you know?"

I knew. What I did not know, however, was when my family's blows or kisses were coming. What I did not know, and could not learn, was who I was. Villain or hero, good boy or bad. Which? What I did learn early in life was that I was a Blechman, and that to be a Blechman was to be *somebody,* a social and financial force in the world. My father owned a large dry goods store in Manhattan. It seemed that my parents viewed everybody as either above or below us, which left us Blechmans on a thin and very lonely rung on the social ladder. This social ladder, I was to discover, was a shaky one. I was born a Jew, and the Nazis had come to power in Germany. The crash of Crystal Night reached Flatbush, and to my ears it was a frightening, bewildering sound. What did it mean? Could it be bad to be a Jew? There was no question that it was a disadvantage. To be a Jew was to be deprived of eating bacon, lettuce, and tomato sandwiches (except when my Aunt Kitty took me to the lunch counter at a neighborhood drugstore). Being a Jew was to be denied the pleasure of having milk or malteds with meat. It was to forego the glitter of Christmas for the sobriety of Chanukah. It was, perhaps worst of all, to be condemned to hard labor at Hebrew School for five afternoons a week (to be released only when it was too dark to play outside!). So being a Jew was no good

thing—a fact recognized by adults who commented approvingly that I looked like a *shagitz* (translation: a Christian). Yiddish was the code my parents used to discuss us, although I soon learned to crack the dialect's key words: *gelt*—money and *kino*—movie.

So I grew up, a *shagitz*-Jew on the Blechman rung of a Flatbush ladder. A problem. If my family name gave no indication of who I was, my first name gave even less. I was born Oscar, but the taunts of my schoolmates soon made me look for a less exotic name. Aunt Kitty found it in short order. I became "Buddy," as in Buddy Rich, Buddy Rogers, and Buddy Ebsen. But "Buddy" was to last only until I opened the heavy oak doors of P. S. 193, where I was known by my middle name Robert, which was mysteriously transposed to become my first name. Only when the school bell sounded did it toll the knell of Robert and signal the rebirth of Buddy. But that was to be my name only too briefly. Daily at four o'clock when I opened the ornate brass doors of the East Midwood Jewish Center, I became "Oysher," the Hebrew form of Oscar. It was not until many years later, as a young man starting his career as a professional artist, that I decided once and for all to settle the matter of my first name. I decided to have none at all. I became "R. O." Occupying a ladder all my own, aloof and unassailable, I felt safe from further transmutations.

But before R. O. was created, Buddy/Oscar/Oysher/Robert lumbered about. In the Flatbush maze, I/we/they desperately sought an exit.

Shoe-box movies provided one escape. Real movies provided another. But real movies cost twenty-five cents—more than half my week's allowance. Moreover, I could go only on Saturdays when children's matinees were held. Clearly, cheaper and more accessible escapes had to be found.

It was Uncle Wiggily who opened the door of literature to me. My brother refused to keep rereading Uncle Wiggily's adventures to me. "*Again?!*" he exclaimed, so I was forced to learn how to read the words myself. They came slowly at first, the *he*'s and *we*'s and

when's painfully joined to the *muskrats, poodle doggies,* and *tar kettles.* But soon the words and meanings flowed together, faster and with increasing ease, and in a few days I could read "It had a turnip steering wheel" as easily as Nurse Jane Fuzzy Wuzzy said, "Well, mercy me, sakes alive, and chocolate drops!" I read *Uncle Wiggily & His Friends* by myself, all the way to its superfluous final passage: "Now Boys and Girls, if you like Uncle Wiggily stories ask your Mother or Daddy to get you a copy of *Uncle Wiggily's Story Book.*" Ask my mother or daddy? I *demanded!* In no time at all I read the thirty-six adventures of *Uncle Wiggily's Story Book.* Then the sequel. Soon the series. Before long there were no new Uncle Wiggilys to be read. Like a young army intoxicated with its new power and flushed with victory, I went on to conquer Doctor Doolittles; next the Rover Boys; then all the Tom Swifts I could find. Everything fell before my invincible eyes. A literary Napoleon, nothing was beyond me, no book in my parents' shelves fazed or frightened me. Hendrik Willem Van Loon's *Lives;* Charles Lindbergh's *We; The Encyclopedia Americana, TAT–UZZ*—I swept through them all. Words, mere (and glorious!) words, I learned to read and spell every one, the bigger the better, the biggest the best. I was the first person on my block not only to know the longest word in the English language, but also to be able to spell it. *Antidisestablishmentarianism.* I think I even knew its meaning. I studied encyclopedias and dared my friends to "ask me a question, any question." I sat on the curb of Twenty-sixth Street, reading until the sun set and the words blurred in the growing darkness and I heard my mother in the distance shouting that my lamb chops were getting cold and I would not get dessert if I did not come home immediately. I left the curb, slowly, pausing by each street lamp, reluctant to leave the bright world of reading for the unbearable dullness of my lighted home.

"For the unbearable dullness of my lighted home." I pause to reconsider this judgment. Was life so dreadful that it had to be fled as if with knotted sheets from a prison or braided hair from a tower? Was life really so difficult? No, it was not, in fact. My life was in many ways privileged, and if the Depression was a grim reality to others, it did not affect the family of S. Blechman & Sons, Dry Goods Wholesalers. From my father's 10-story building, as if from a stone-and-brick cornucopia, flowed doctor's kits with pink candy pills, fringed cowboy suits, and—most precious gifts of all!—booklets of ribbon samples. Pinks, lilacs, creams, mauves . . . emerald greens, Kelly greens, mint greens, jade greens. . . . The tiny squares of colored velvet set in their cardboard pages were like jewels in a relic. Surprinted on the cover was a crimson "S. Blechman & Sons." Below it I proudly added "Buddy." The Christmas I was denied once a year came several days a week except on Saturdays when the store was closed for *Shabbas* (a practice instituted by my grandfather, and followed, probably half-heartedly, by my less religious, but still respectful, father).

No, life was not a prison. In the summer I escaped the heat of Flatbush for the cool mountains of Camp Cascade or Berkshire Pines. My first summer away was spent at a "family camp," separated from my parents only by a clay-red road, splotched with the bodies of frogs (Nature was prodigal then, so rich with varied and beautiful creatures that there was always life to spare). In the evening I crossed the splattered path to join my parents in the adult lodge. My father was dressed in deep-pleated linen trousers and a V-neck sweater. My mother wore an extravagantly flowered dress. She was seated at the piano, her face lifted and her madder-tipped fingers descending. "When the deep purple falls. . . . " The music flowed toward me, *dripping over sleepy garden walls, slipping under silver lagoons, and the mist began to gather in the night.* Bliss!

My second summer away was spent at a children's camp, without my parents. Unbearable separation! Camp was merely half a heaven. My third summer was heaven quartered. Away from my parents, this new camp alternated between fairy tale and horror story with a Grimm Brothers' perversity. It was at once the best-of-all-possible-worlds—and the worst. It was the carriage turning into a pumpkin, the prince to a toad, the dream to a nightmare—all with such startling, frequent, and unexpected shifts that it seemed as if

My father and his cousin William in Atlantic City, 1925.

A booklet from The House of Blechman.

My father as a wooden drummer en route to Germany on the *S.S. President Fillmore,* 1923.

a fairy's wand had gone berserk. My camp counselors were Uncle Tom and Uncle Alfred. Uncle Tom was tall, thin, and hawk-nosed. Uncle Alfred was round and wore thick glasses. Both were homosexuals. "Get undressed!" they ordered a child when his unmade bed had caused our bunk to fail inspection. "Get undressed!" The offender had to march from the bunk, across the long parade field, and into the mess hall. Getting undressed was a more drastic punishment than "Kiss my Dicky Boy!," which was at least not a public spectacle.

Set on the edge of a glistening northern lake, the lodges were built in the Adirondacks style of cedar logs on boulder bases. Every morning fires blazed in the massive stone fireplaces to offset the mountain cold. After marching to the flagpole and pledging allegiance to the flag of the United States of America and to the Republic for Which It Stands, we marched briskly to the mess hall where our paramilitary formations broke up and we could be chaotically "at ease." Breakfasts were hearty; we had hot or cold cereal, griddle cakes with syrup or eggs (any style) or both, and toast and/or corn and bran muffins, milk and/or hot cocoa—singles, doubles, triples—whatever our promiscuous appetites demanded, however bizarre the combination or excessive the amount we wanted, we received. We were, for that giddy stretch of time, as free as adults. Uncle Tom and Uncle Alfred minded only our manners.

The climax of our feasting came at the end of the Blue and White War. After fruit salad with sherbet, grilled steaks with gravy, baked potatoes bursting with sour cream and chives, the green-shaded overhead lamps grew dim. Suddenly, emerging from the darkened kitchen area, a flickering blue light appeared. Then another, and another. The blue flames moved toward us until they were close enough for us to recognize that these were our waiters bearing silver trays of flaming—flaming what? The lights went on. "Baked Alaska!" Uncle Alfred announced. He blew out the flames, cut the cake, and passed out the portions. We were dumbfounded. Inside

the fiery crust, ice cream! We were Columbus, landing in Cathay, but discovering it was America. At the time the symbolism of this flaming yet frigid dish escaped me. It was 1938, and Freud was still in Vienna, unknown to most Americans and unmentioned in my *Encyclopedia Americana.* We suffered in ignorance then.

Toward the end of August, we took a three-day trip to nearby Canada. We stayed at an army camp (the symbolism of which also escaped me), swapping our dollars for the soldiers' more exotic-looking ones. On the last evening we had our chance to spend them. We marched to the nearby town and bought Canadian postcards, Canadian pennants with outsized maple leaves, Canadian sandwiches and milk shakes, and visited a Canadian movie house where we saw Tyrone Power ("Is *he* Canadian?") die a Technicolor death in *Blood and Sand.* The glory of it all! The glory was to vanish the next morning. We returned to our camp, and Tyrone Power and the Canadian army were replaced by Uncles Tom and Alfred and "Get undressed!" The baked Alaska was a fraud. Inside was more fire.

I tried to tell my parents about summer camp, but Uncle Alfred read all outgoing mail. I managed to smuggle one letter past him, but my parents must have read it with disbelief. They signed me up for the next season. Two weeks before camp began I settled the matter. While playing shuffleboard at Jones Beach I broke my toe.

A child tends to turn everything inward, to consider himself, and himself alone, responsible for whatever happens to his life. I felt responsible for the punishments Uncle Tom and Uncle Alfred meted out and for the rebuffs of my mother. Could they—adults—be wrong, and I—a child—be right? I had been—no doubt about it—a bad boy, or at least an irrepressible, unruly boy, and therefore a bad one in the eyes of the schoolmarm world. What else could explain the behavior of a child who would suddenly walk up to Frances Walters, the prettiest girl in the gym class, kiss her on the mouth, and calmly return to his place in the now zig-zagging line? Who else but an

Mother
and Father in Havana, 1927.

Manhattan, circa 1940.

outrageous kind of child would act this way?

But perhaps—on reconsideration—and I am, if nothing else, a person who reconsiders, a man who always thinks, "now on the other hand," which is why God gave me two of them—perhaps my kissing Frances Walters was not so much the action of a bad child as it was the action of an insecure child who desperately needed to attract the attention he could never receive consistently from his mother or fully from his father.

Whatever the explanation, I decided at age 10 or so that I would no longer be "a bad boy"; it was just not working. I was no happier being a bad boy than an ordinary one. I decided to become a good boy. As with all converts to anything, my conversion to good behavior was not half-hearted. I became not merely a good boy, but a model good boy, a too-good-to-be-true good boy. So my fisted hands left their pockets. They were brought together for what I intended to be a lifelong clasp. In many ways I succeeded, because I am still, at age 50, trying to unclasp them.

In 1941, while my brother and I were watching Errol Flynn shoot the Cheyennes in the Elm Theatre, the Japanese bombed Pearl Harbor. A year later the exigencies of gas rationing forced us to move to Manhattan where S. Blechman & Sons was located.

Manhattan. I cried the first night we were there. But Manhattan taught lessons that would hold and nourish for a lifetime. The city was an open-ended classroom. I was its wandering, open-eyed auditor. On Sunday nights I went to Columbus Circle, then closed to traffic. Dozens of speakers gathered there, each with his own tight knot of listeners, arguing the way of Trotsky, Marx, Fundamentalism, vitamin B_1, and atheism. Talk flowed as fully and freely as the water gushing from the square's monument to the *Maine*. The harangues continued until late at night when the speakers left, but their audiences would not, breaking into smaller, still arguing, groups. Could any school have provided such a passionate and varied forum as this? Alone in the night, reluctant to leave for home, I wandered down to Bryant Park where, for ten cents, I viewed the full moon and learned the names of every one of its craters and crests (I passed up the canals of Mars and the rings of Venus, which cost a quarter). During the day I walked through narrow passageways on Third Avenue and entered garden courtyards filled with antique shops displaying *tankas*, tapestries, decoys, Delft chargers, cigar-store Indians, baskets heaped with Flemish lace, Coptic fragments, and Renaissance damasks. These courtyards were my *stoa*, and I learned by touch and by sight my first lessons in history, art, and anthropology. Books could never replace, nor museums duplicate, these tangible lessons.

Eye level with the shiny finials of Mercury (New York's God of Commerce, whose effigy blessed the city on the façade of Grand Central Terminal) topping each elegant Deco traffic light, I rode the tops of open-decked Fifth Avenue buses (always the top and always up front). "Go the Motor Coach Way," their signs said, in slanted Twenties script. But was there any other way? Was there any other way to see the buildings, the granite-blocked mansions, and the steel-trimmed skyscrapers than from above and in the open, so that the city could be experienced like a vast Cubist sculpture, from all sides and simultaneously? And was there any better way to experience a skyscraper than to see it scrape the sky? If not from an open-topped bus, then from a "Sky Top" Checker, an elevated train, or a convertible. Manhattan was my school without a book, my *alma mater*, my *magna mater*, and I absorbed the lessons with wonder and boundless gratitude.

The lessons ended at the doors of junior high school. Miss Goldstein, my music appreciation teacher, stood slightly less than five feet tall in her Enna Jetticks, slightly taller with her raised baton. It descended twice a week for "Country Gardens" and "D'Ye Ken John Peel?" Perhaps because of her diminutive size we were told several times a month that she had grown up only two doors down from Tommy Dorsey. Our art teacher was Miss Ohara (sic), who had us copy *National Geographic* photographs with our Crayolas. World War II had just begun, and our subjects were Friendly Natives of the Micronesias, Anthracite Coal Fights for Victory, and The Yangtze: China's Main Street. My Crayola copies bore little re-

book illustration by
Maxa Nordau.

Leonard Bernstein in
his twenties.

semblance to the originals. It seemed evident that the artistic talent of Aunt Kitty and Uncle Nat had been lost somehow in the genetic scramble.

While I was still in junior high school, my mother asked me to take the entrance examination for the High School of Music and Art. One of several highly specialized public schools, Music and Art offered an intensive course in either music or art along with a standard academic curriculum. Admission to the school was highly competitive. I was not sure whether my mother meant me to enter as a music or an art student because I was equally unqualified and disinterested in both. "Art," she said, with the blind faith that only a mother could have in the face of all evidence to the contrary. My brother was clearly more an artist than I was. It was he who copied a Marsden Hartley waterfall from *Life* magazine with such fidelity that at first glance it seemed as if there had been a dreadful mistake, and that Malatzky & Son had framed the *Life* page instead of the canvas. It was my brother who took a sculpture class every Saturday at the Art Students League and filled our room with marble chips during the week. It was he who was the artist, but through some terrible error, it was I who took the examination. What was evident to everybody else was not so clear to my mother.

I prepared my portfolio with the help of a neighbor, Maxa Nordau, a painter who had left her native Paris at the outbreak of the war. Madame Nordau was an evocation of Parisian grace: She was pale, blond, slender, her blue eyes set off by lavender eye shadow and contrasted with an exceedingly pointed nose. She lived with her mother, a tall and stately lady; a plumpish daughter, Claudie; and a man whom I had great difficulty in reconciling as her husband. He was short, stolid, and wore thick, dark suits. The two of them seemed to be the pairing of an iridescent Gallé dragonfly with a no-nonsense bee. Clearly a match not made in heaven.

Madame Nordau had decorated her apartment which faced Central Park with murals that brought the gay greens and earth colors of the park into her home. Among the trees, bowed bridges, and Gothic chalets of the park were such unconventional notes as a donkey with its tail strategically placed on the light switch of her wall. Entering her home from my blue-gray apartment, carefully decorated in a Shanghai Chippendale style, I felt it was like entering an artist's Left Bank studio. Our apartments were only several feet, but many worlds, apart.

Madame Nordau's help was only incidentally technical. It more often took the form of a smile, a nod, a graceful wave of the hand to dispel my anxieties about the world that lay beyond the known and familiar confines of my magazine rack.

On the subway to Music and Art, I had no apprehensions about the examination. It did not matter, really, if I passed or failed. What mattered more was that the examination be short, and that I return in time for the 2:30 Dodgers' game. Several weeks later I learned that I had passed. I neglected to tell my parents about it immediately because it did not seem important enough to mention at the dinner table.

Barely a decade old, Music and Art already had a tradition. It had produced a Miss America, Bess Myerson, and a film star, Tommy Dix, whose rendition of "Buckle Down, Winsockee" was number one on the Hit Parade. Number One! We felt we were all Number Ones. It was 1944. The war, whose outcome was so uncertain at first, was drawing to a successful close. The Bomb was yet to fall and cast its permanent shadow over our lives. The future was bright, and it was ours. It was signified by a special event.

Although it was a senior-class assembly, word of the concert spread throughout the school. As the news reached each classroom, students left, at first singly, giving the classic excuse of having to go to the bathroom; then in pairs, saying nothing; and finally in bold groups. The teachers at first gave their uneasy acquiescence to the evacuation, then their active encouragement. Within fifteen minutes the senior assembly was packed with

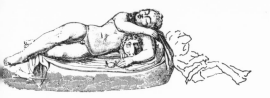

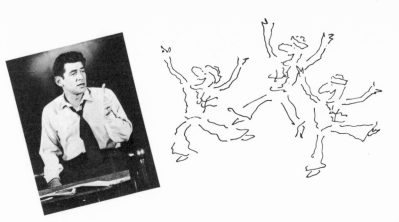

seated, squatting, and standing students, all waiting to greet the 26-year-old protégé of Koussevitzky and composer of "On the Town"—Leonard Bernstein, who had agreed to conduct our orchestra. For two hours the school was on a self-proclaimed holiday, not only to celebrate Leonard Bernstein but to celebrate ourselves as well. His presence signified our importance, acknowledged our specialness. We were, Bernstein and us—like his three sailors on Broadway—about to conquer New York. Nothing less.

As it happened, few of us went on to capture anything. What we did capture, and spectacularly, was the High School of Music and Art itself, with brilliant productions of art, music, and theater. Perhaps, like bright rockets, we burned ourselves out in a too-rapid display of our pyrotechnic abilities. Those who went on to success after Music and Art were not the luminaries in school. It was the lesser lights who were to become the lasting ones.

My art teacher was Miss Oakman. Her first assignment was a snow scene. How I labored on it with the unfamiliar temperas, dipping my brush in the tree-brown, carefully dunking it clean, passing on to the snow-white, then the face—mixing the red with the white and, why not?, a touch of yellow, then on to the snowsuit-blue, the mittens-red, the galoshes-brown, all the time dunking, lips pursed in a good-boy effort which was soon forgotten as my blue boy was joined by yellow-and-green friends sludging through the fresh-fallen snow getting deeper as the afternoon advanced and the large white flakes fell ever thicker over suits, faces, mittens, hats. . . .

Done! "Now sign them," she said, "and bring them to the front table." A moment's hesitation. A sudden decision. "Blechman" I signed—no first name (a tabula rasa for my new life in school)—and brought it to her desk, where it was soon covered by a heavy fall of snow scenes. She took the pile and, one by one, thumbtacked them on the corkboard running the length of the room. One group of paintings was pinned on the far left of the board. To the right, separated by an emphatic wood divider, a second group of paintings was hung. She turned toward us, her cultivated Australian face an absolute deadpan. What was she going to say? What did the separation of the paintings mean? Was it the chaff from the wheat, the dross from the gold, the damned from the blessed? Agony!

"Now, these show promise," she said, waving her hand in the direction of one group. "They show imagination. And these—" she hesitated. How damning was her well-bred hesitation! I filled in her lacunae with the severest criticism—"these show less quality than I would like."

Less quality than she would like! Her judgment was made. It was final, unquestionable, unalterable. It came with all the authority that a British accent had to Brooklyn ears. I got up from my chair to see which side of the Last Judgment I was on. Triumph! I was among the Blessed Who Show Promise, the Few Who Show Imagination. "These have a sense of composition . . . a feeling for color . . ." she went on, but it hardly mattered, these descriptions of the beatific glow. What mattered was that among the Blessed I had a place! Miss Oakman's praise set me up with an image of myself that was to serve me well in the semester ahead.

A Saint Anthony in the first semester, I was sorely tested in the desert of my second semester. The test was to take the form of a small and constantly changing object placed on a stool against an unvarying drape. "Draw it," Miss Oakman commanded, "care-ful-ly." *Où sont les neiges d'antan?* Gone were the carefree days drawn from scenes of my imagination. They were replaced by the nightmare shades of reality. The hard lines of still lifes had replaced the soft shapes of the mind, and there was to be no smudging reality with a pen line or a 2H. "Draw it." The "it" could be an apple, a bottle, or a hat, but they all had in common one awful fact. They seemed to be symmetrical. Once I was able to tame one side of the object and fix it onto the pad, the other side resisted all efforts to be tamed. Like a refractory horse resisting the yoke of his partner; like a Siamese twin walking left to his brother's right; like one eye perversely crossing the other; either side of the damned symmetrical object would stubbornly resist all my efforts to get it to be-

have like the other side.

Soon my drawings moved from the Blessed side of the corkboard to that of the Damned. My grades moved accordingly. The A I received in the first semester ("See!" my mother had said. "And you didn't want to take the exam!") changed to a C— and threatened to descend even lower. My mother was silent, unbelieving. Madame Nordau waved her hand, but it was wandless. My spirits sank fast, threatening to disappear beneath the bubbling waters of my brother's waterfall, hanging in our room like a daily reproach.

I stayed afloat. The next semester the stool went into the supply room along with its display of torture instruments, and we reverted to subjects from our imagination. Gone as well were the companion tools of torture, the pen and the 2H. They were replaced by soft sable brushes and cakes of Winsor & Newton watercolor. That semester I discovered a medium that has remained a lifelong delight.

Unique among the visual mediums, watercolor requires instant decisions. Once made, they cannot be unmade. As soon as the wash is put down, it has to be left, moved, mixed, thinned, blended, or collected to form an accent—all within seconds, before the color dries permanently. To a repressed boy, this possibility of spontaneous action afforded precious bursts of freedom. To an indecisive boy, it was a joy to have to act without the possibility of reconsideration or revision. Besides the spontaneity of watercolor, I cherish its translucence, its brilliance, its exquisitely subtle and startlingly dramatic modulations from light to dark, wet to dry, bright to dull, limpid to dense, all of which no other medium can obtain.

I loved watercolor above all mediums. When I was not at the Museum of Modern Art, arched in front of a George Grosz, I was in the Weyhe Gallery, bent over a John Marin that I had just pulled from a drawer full of his watercolors. Or I was at the Subway Gallery, leafing through a portfolio thick with Rodin drawings (at one hundred dollars apiece;

or the price of a year's supply of butter pecan ice cream, my nightly indulgence).

But despite my love for watercolor, I neither wanted to be an artist nor thought of myself as one. Enjoyable as it was (when it did not involve a still life), it did not sufficiently connect with that more restless life that throbbed in my bulging head. What intrigued me, challenged me, taunted and often tormented me were ideas and feelings—and feelings far more than ideas—that could not be tapped by images alone. Something else was needed, some other form had to be found. But which? Did it even exist? "Where was the place God intended for me when he made me thus awry?"

The place God intended for me may have been no more than four blocks away. The Thalia was an art-film theater, the first in Manhattan, and one of only a few in the country during the Forties. Short and narrow, more like an aisle than an auditorium, it could have fitted easily in the lobby of any nearby movie palace. Its size suited its role, that of a revolutionary cell burrowed in the superstructure of an industry dedicated to family entertainment on the vastest and shallowest scale.

At the Thalia I first saw Marcel Pagnol's *Marius* and experienced the small and homely truths that I had never encountered in Andy Hardy—fathered as much by the deceitful Hay's Code as by the upright Judge Hardy; I met up with the grandeur and moral sweep of Marcel Carne's *Le Jour se Lève* and Jean Renoir's *La Grande Illusion*, and experienced the exquisite and extravagant fantasy of René Clair's *A Nous la Liberté*. Slanted in my steeply pitched seat at the Thalia, gazing up as if toward heaven, these filmmakers and their masterpieces were a revelation I would never forget. I later painted a mural of heaven and hell for a college dance. The centerpiece of heaven was the Universal Theater showing Sergei Eisenstein's *Alexander Nevsky*. Its marquee read "Admission—free, Performances—forever." Heaven, indeed!

I was not entirely unprepared for these films. As an 11-year-old

I had gone to Manhattan with my brother to see *Citizen Kane*. We were so electrified by the film that taking a subway home was out of the question. Not right away, at least. We had to walk. On the way we passed Gimbel's where an entire street of its windows were displaying the massive furnishings of William Randolph Hearst's San Simeon, recently bought by the store. Farther down Broadway we came to the army and navy store of Bannerman (who owned a Gothic castle, now a shell on its Hudson River island). In its window were Springfield rifles and regimental banners from the very war Kane had so gustily promoted in the film. The whole world seemed to confirm the truth of *Citizen Kane* as it reflected the larger-than-life vision of his creator, and my brother and I, unable to forsake this vast living theater for a dark, crabbed subway, walked all the way home to Flatbush. Rosebud.

I also went often to the Museum of Modern Art film library. On Thursday nights, I entered the chapel-sized theater, moving toward the seats closest to the screen and farthest from people, as if human contact were a profanation. Communion with the film was all that mattered. (I am not by nature a social person, but in theaters I am positively misanthropic.) I lowered the seat and waited, deeply slouched, for the lights to dim and the ceremony to begin. Silently, austerely, the film notes appeared on the screen, majestically ascending, lifting with them all the cares of my day. Rapidly reading the lines, I would reread the previous ones, reluctant to leave them before they disappeared forever, taking comfort in them as a celebrant would in the catechism.

When the film ended, when the too-brief ceremony concluded, when the too-bright lights went on, and the too-noisy audience rose to leave, I made my way to the exit, keeping my distance from everybody, a somnambulist. Nothing was real to me except what I had just experienced with all the depths of my being. These shadows on the screen—they were real—and what they said and did—that was real. It was Plato's allegory of the cave, but *only* the shadows existed; nothing else.

Back home, the words came—the intrusions—the insistent shaking of my shoulders to rouse me from the dream too sweet to leave. "Where did you? . . . What did? . . . homework . . . Grandma. . . . " I could barely acknowledge my parents' words. I wanted to lie on my bed, in the dark which was the dark of the theater, and relive the moments that were richer and truer than anything life had to offer.

It never occurred to me that one day *I* might make films. It seemed beyond desire—like a cripple wanting to race when he could not even walk—that I might follow in the paths of those who were my saints. But it was toward film that I was heading. In my own way. At my own pace. According to my own clock, faceless and silently ticking at a pace that was so slow I sensed no movement at all and that I was sure did not exist.

Just as shoe-box movies were my childhood substitute for films I could not afford, picture-and-story books became my substitute for films I could not make. The stories took the form of booklets, lovingly sewn together. Each drawing, accompanied by a brief text, usually occupied a full page, but sometimes they were a double or half a page, or several or many drawings on a page, depending on how fast or slowly I wanted to move along an action. The considerations were wholly cinematic, although I was unaware of this at the time.

My subjects were profound and flighty, passionate and flip, about what mattered most or mattered the least to me: a trip to Nantucket (which mattered a lot); a thank-you note for a Bar Mitzvah gift—a lot for the suede-and-silk vest I wore to spotted tatters; a little for the twenty-five-dollar defense bond. Everything in life became the occasion and the excuse, the trigger and the target for my booklets.

Perhaps (Always "perhaps"! "Daddy," my older son once said to me, resenting the ambiguity of my answers to him, "tell me 'Yes' or tell me 'No,' but please don't tell me 'Maybe.' "), perhaps my need to encapsulate life in booklets was my way of controlling its capriciousness, what I sensed to be its danger. My mother was a

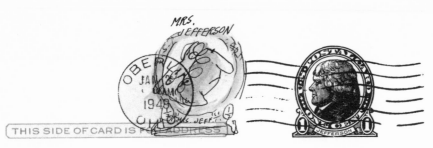

most unpredictable lady, and maybe she is at the heart (ah, the heart!) of my need to formulate, to fix, things—to carve a little order out of the bewildering and dangerous disorder that surrounded and might otherwise turn against me.

I have always preferred the shadows (of every sort) to the light, the sideways glance to the direct look. Is it any wonder, given my penchant for indirection, that I chose to communicate through pictures and text rather than actions and speech? These booklets were my hands to a world I feared to touch. They were my tongues for words I could not say. What I could not speak, I wrote, and what I could not write in earnest, I wrote and drew in jest. In jest? How could I otherwise mask the hatred and the fear bred of my loneliness? And what better way to mitigate the loneliness than to attract an audience (safely and necessarily distant)?

I chose to act out much of my life on paper, where I was to pass its most heightened moments.

"Heaven and Hell," the mural I had painted for the college dance, had taken me an entire night to paint. When the dance came, I did not go. Why go? I was already there in the far superior form of my art. How the organdy-gowned girls admired me, how the buckskin-shoed boys envied me, as they danced cheek to cheek but with eyes up, down, and around, for me alone. "Full Moon," the orchestra played, "and Empty Arms . . . ," yes, but my head was as full as any moon could be with the steady and intense glow of reflected warmth. From my lonely rung on the ladder, perched against the wall of the makeshift ballroom, I had made contact with the world.

It was 1948. I was at Oberlin College, then an institution far removed from its feminist and radical abolitionist origins (the first college to admit a woman; the first to admit a black). After the effervescence of Music and Art, Oberlin seemed as bland as the 3.2 beer it was legally permitted to serve. The minds and spirits of the student body seemed to move as horizontally as its Ohio setting and patois, and to this manic New Yorker, racing his bike on the streets banned to student cars, there seemed nowhere to go.

Oberlin proclaimed itself a Christian college, and saying grace was for me a painful feature of Sunday dinner. Grace was followed by the singing of the doxology, "Praise God from Whom all blessings flow," which I had learned to mouth silently, eyes lowered on the fruit salad down which flowed the pink ball of raspberry sherbet. By the time "Praise Father, Son, and Holy Ghost" was reached, the pink ice had become runny water somewhere in my cup, and my brow was streaming.

Compulsory chapel was held every Wednesday noon, another reminder that Oberlin was not my world. Of course no place, really, could be "my world." But the Christian cast of Oberlin was particularly disturbing to somebody who could neither belong to it nor entirely resist it. I might have been better off with a black skullcap and earlocks to match. At least then Betty Ann Miller, walking with me across the elm-lined path of the quadrangle, would not have asked "what" I was. It must have been evident that I was not at all comfortable with "What I was" (but then, I was not comfortable with anything).

Also on Wednesdays, the school newspaper was delivered to the dining halls. I noticed that the *Oberlin Review* had one obvious omission. The *New York Post* had Herblock; the *Herald Tribune*, Dowling; *PM*, Saul Steinberg. But the *Oberlin Review* had—who? I turned its eight pages and found no cartoon. I waited for the next issue, and still saw no cartoon. It was clear that a need existed, theirs and mine, which had to be filled. Since my nature abhorred an artistic vacuum, I offered to fill it. The editor, knowing a free thing when he saw it, accepted.

Every week I drew a political cartoon for the newspaper. The sometimes rich ideas must have lost something from the rather tattered visual forms I clothed them in. I remember one classmate remarking, "Buddy, if you could only draw as well as you talk." Well, I didn't, and it wasn't important either. What was more important than drawing well was thinking well, and when that happened it seemed accomplishment enough.

A postcard to a high-school classmate.

At Oberlin, 1948.

At the Oberlin Arch (dedicated to the martyrs of the Boxer Rebellion), 1948.

The Oberlin bookstore.

In the army, 1953.

The United Nations Secretariat Building had just been constructed, and New Yorkers admired the novelty of the glass structure. There was less to admire in the structure of the organization itself. Torn by an intensifying East-West feud, the United Nations was powerless to check the arms race and the conflicts erupting throughout the world. I drew a two-panel cartoon of the building, labeling it "The United Nations" (in case my drawing didn't read): "The Last Resort." The first panel showed the glass exterior, the second showed the delegates in an endless line of deck chairs, sunning themselves in their new glass house. It never occurred to me that people in glass houses should not throw stones. In pointing out the delegates' hypocrisy, I was happy to ignore my own.

Shortly after becoming the staff cartoonist of the *Review*, I gave it up to become the newspaper's movie critic. Every week I passionately argued the merits and demerits of films the Apollo Theatre was about to play. "About to play." Had I seen them, then, in previews? No, but as the old saw goes, I didn't read the book, but I did read the reviews. "No," I answered Professor Hoover, my English teacher, when he asked me about this, "I didn't see the films, but I did read the reviews. In the *Cleveland Plain Dealer*, and—the *New York Times*—and—" (reaching high)—"the *New Republic*." A week later I resigned the post of movie reviewer.

After two years at Oberlin, where my major had become History and my minor English, I restlessly transferred to the newly established Department of Graphic Arts at Columbia University. But a year of studying Clarendon, Bodoni, and Cheltenham typefaces, and not knowing the clear differences, and not caring either, made me look back to Oberlin. I returned there for my senior year.

This constant changing of venue, real or theoretical, has been a feature of my life. The grass has always seemed greener elsewhere. This restlessness has led me to abandon many projects midway through them. However, it has also driven me beyond accepting the easy, "apparent" solution to a problem to finding the more difficult, but richer solution. When an art director of an advertising agency presents me with a layout, I invariably modify the concept. This is more than a perversity or idiosyncrasy: only the person who executes a job can see it most clearly. If "God is in the details," as Mies van der Rohe remarks, then God—or perfection—can only come from the final working out of these details (although sometimes the first brilliant flash of a notion fades in the tedious working out of it, and the sketch must be returned to as the basis for the finish).

Until very recently I had a recurring dream. I was wandering in Manhattan and came across an area that I had never seen before. It was thickly wooded, with streams and rolling hills. In the dream I could never understand how I could have lived in Manhattan for so long and not known of this secret pocket.

I once mentioned the dream to my brother (who by now had become a novelist), and he remarked that he, too, often had the same dream. What could it mean, this image of a veritable Eden within the strident city? Could it be, in Jungian terms, the archetypal dream of a Promised Land? Or could it be, more simply, my awareness of another way of life? Mine for the mere walking? Perhaps my obsession to look beyond whatever I have is a symbolic way of walking toward this life. "Perhaps. Always perhaps," my children would say.

In 1952 I was graduated from Oberlin. It was not a cold world that I entered, but the increasingly hot one of the Korean War. The Chinese had just entered the war, and our troops were retreating in what seemed more and more like a rout. The draft was intensifying, and it was only a matter of time before I would enter the army and probably be sent to the Far East. I decided to spend my time doing what I wanted to, however impractical. Nothing could have been more impractical than becoming a professional illustrator. My style—such as it was—had no precedents, and therefore no clear outlets.

But it was my good fortune that at this time all notions of draftsmanship and the role of the illustrator were changing. Prior to the Fifties, illustration was considered merely a handmaiden to the text

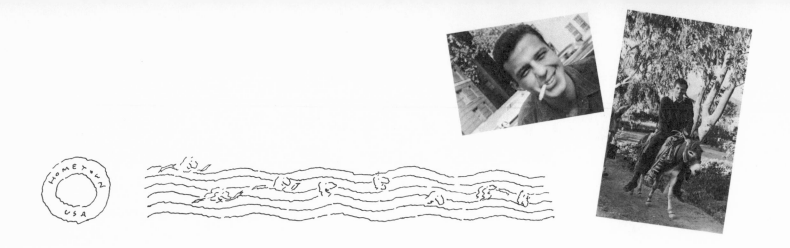

that accompanied it; a junior partner in the firm, good looking but not overly ambitious or competitive to the senior partner. If a line read, "Bill kissed Sally in the hammock as it swayed gently between the hemlocks," the illustrator's job was strictly to render Bill kissing Sally in the hammock as it swayed gently (not vigorously!) between the hemlocks (not pines!). It was not for illustration to aspire to the status of literature as Anton Chekhov described it: "The moon reflected in a piece of glass at the bottom of a stream." Illustration was the moon, period. Or the glass, period. Nothing less, and nothing more—no reflections, no distortions. But this was changing. The key word in the Fifties was "concept"—the idea that almost alone justified the illustration. A godsend to a person like myself, who could not bear to accept any given situation, but had to look compulsively elsewhere for one, and who had considerable difficulties anyway rendering hammocks and hemlocks.

Along with this new emphasis on conceptual freedom was an impatience with stylistic literalness. The pendulum was swinging away from Norman Rockwell and other *Saturday Evening Post* illustrators toward more stylized looks. Typical of these was the "stitched" line, a jagged, or barbed, highly self-conscious line. (Although even the most casual lines are self-conscious in the sense that the artist is both aware of his or her effect and strives mightily to achieve it. The split-pen line of the *New Yorker* cartoonist George Price seems to be the accidental effect of increased pressure on the flexible pen point. In fact, it is painted white to resemble the splaying of a pen point.)

It was on this cresting wave of concept and stylization that I moved into the illustration world. My very inability to draw easily (but I know of few artists who draw "easily," despite either the assurance or the casualness of their work) made me put more demands on content and humor, qualities that were to serve me well.

In the pre-television, pre-paperback days of the early Fifties, magazines were still vehicles for mass entertainment and communication. Brentano's could devote its entire basement floor to magazines. It was in the basement of Brentano's that I sought out the names of small-circulation, highly illustrated publications as the most likely prospects for my work. One of these magazines was *Park East,* a cross between *New York* and *Cue* magazines. The editors gave me my first professional assignment, a full page on the subject of my choice. A full page! The subject of *my* choice! I was overwhelmed. My family was spending the summer in a rented house near the seashore, so my eyes were full of beach scenes, my ears with beach conversations. There was no problem in finding a subject. It was there, all around me. The problem, rather, was in finding a way to draw it. It seemed clear to me that the art director could not like my style as much as suffer it for the sake of my ideas and humor. I resolved to give him his money's worth by resolutely copying a popular style of illustration. I drew "A Day at the Beach" in the "stitched" line technique. I copied it so well that I did not feel at all unworthy of the check I received several weeks later. (And which I could hardly bear to cash. Everybody had money, but how many people had one-hundred-dollar checks made out to them by *Park East* magazine?)

My next assignment was a Christmas gift subscription form for *Theatre Arts* magazine. I decided to abandon my "stitched" line technique for my own way of drawing. My work for *Park East* was the first and last excursion into the styles of other artists.

My portfolio at the time consisted mostly of work done at Oberlin: posters, cartoons from the newspaper, illustrations from the literary magazine, several neatly sewn booklets, and one picture story set in Rome called *Titus*. "Can I show that book to a publisher?" a graphics designer, Ben Feder, asked me. I had never really thought of the book as publishable. It was done as a term paper for a workshop class (and received a B−), and I considered this its final incarnation.

Theodore Amussen, then editor-in-chief at Henry Holt, asked if

Out of
the army, 1954.

Vacationing
at Lindos, 1959.

On the terrace of my
first apartment, 1959.

I could do a similar book for him, but based on a holiday theme, "preferably Christmas." Preferably Christmas! If only he had said Halloween or New Year's Eve, I might have been happier, but Christmas! My mind was awash in Christmas notions all year round, and asking me to do something with this holiday was like asking me to dam a piece of the ocean. I was desperate. I telephoned a friend. "Do you know of a good Christmas story?" I asked. To my astonishment, the cry for help was met with instant aid. "The Juggler of Our Lady," he answered. "Do you know it?"

Yes, I knew it. Rereading the legend the next day, I realized that it was precisely the story I wanted. The juggler desperately performing before an indifferent world might have served as the parable of my own life. I knew that this was an ideal story to adapt. I set to work immediately. Clearing the kitchen table of everything but the white paper, and Will Durant's *Age of Faith* as reference, I started the book that evening, and finished it the same night. In the morning I took it to Holt, and it was accepted for publication. An epic event in my life, glorious and tragic! Glorious in the acclaim it was to bring me, tragic in its consequences. Twenty-odd years later I was to learn its significance.

"Success," the psychiatrist's wife explained as we were discussing a mutual friend who had published a highly regarded book years ago, but who had been unable to write anything since, "can be as traumatic as failure. If you are bred to failure, success can come as a terrible shock." "Bred to failure." It is true that I never had much faith in myself. Despite occasional but real successes, I never connected them solidly with myself but considered them as somehow incidental, lucky spins of fate. When *The Juggler of Our Lady* was published and met with great acclaim, I associated success with the book but not with me, whom I considered undeserving. Convinced that success lay in producing other Jugglers, I set out to do more of them. *Son of the Juggler, Grandson of the Juggler, Grand Nieces and Nephews of the Juggler*—I turned them out with Catholic fervor, but to no effect. They were stillborn, all. In the meantime the years went by, and, still desperately trying to produce offspring—*Cousin of the Juggler, Bastard of the Juggler*—I would not stop; I could not stop. I did not realize that I was changing from the 22-year-old who had sat down at the kitchen table with a pad of paper, *The Age of Faith*, and a vision. No longer the same person, I could no longer produce the same work.

Years later, when I received offers from France, England, and the United States to reprint the book, I refused them all. I could not bear to reprint it. I saw it as a sign of failure. It was either a new book or nothing. For twelve years, therefore, it was nothing.

Weeks before *The Juggler of Our Lady* was published, I was drafted. This cut short my burgeoning career as illustrator. I was fortunate that it did not cut short my life. Instead of being sent to Korea, which was then in the final paroxysms of war, I was sent to Asbury Park where I swam in the Atlantic every evening after serving my country during the day. Two years later I was discharged. But the return to civilian life was gradual and only diurnal. For almost a year I dreamed nightly that I was still in the army. I don't know why the army was such a shock, considering both how I spent my service and my experience as a child in summer camp, but a shock it was. Perhaps because the army confirmed fearful doubts about myself that had been put to rest during my year as an artist. At basic training camp in Georgia we were never referred to as soldiers. "I want twenty asses to come here on the double!" the NCOs commanded. "Three asses will perform clean-up detail." "Which asses left this gear?" "I want you asses. . . ." Several months of this was enough to cut down my already meager self-confidence. When this ass took the test for Officers' Candidate School, it/he/I failed predictably.

In the spring of 1954, upon my return to civilian life, this ass slept for a week. The sleep was transforming. Miraculously, I sprouted a head, legs, two arms, hands, fingers—I became a human being. It was time to resume this particular human being's identity.

I took my portfolio around to the magazines. My resumed activity can be summarized by a ledger book of freelance work, begun in my father's bold handwriting (the t's not so much crossed as slashed):

INCOME	DATE	SOURCE	EXPLANATION
$100.	3/-/54	U.S. Army #51236476	Separation pay
75.	4/21	Esquire	Illustration
50.63	4/26	Holt	Royalty

Here my father's slashes leave off, and my penciled notations take over:

50.	4/28	RCA Victor	Sketch for album
175.	5/12	RCA Victor	Finish for album
112.40	6/16	John Rawlings	Backdrop
75.	6/18	Grey Advertising	NBC sketch
510.	7/5	Grey Advertising	NBC finishes
350.	6/24	Pageant	Story
75.	7/12	Esquire	Illustration
100.	8/2	Gumbinner	D'Orsay ad

My notations ended with a telephone call. John Hubley, the animator, had seen *The Juggler of Our Lady.* Would I care to work with him as his assistant?

Storyboard, Inc., Hubley's new company, was named after the panels of drawings and text, or "storyboards," which show the continuity of an animated film. It was my job to create storyboards for the commercials that were produced by his West Coast branch. (My style was considered too loose and sketchy for the animation itself.)

For one year I was to graze film with no closer contact. In Jean-Luc Godard's *A Woman Is a Woman* the protagonist is asked, "*Comment ça va?*" "*J'existe,*" is the answer, offered with a shrug. At Storyboard, Inc., I existed, thank you. I worked in a handsome studio two doors away from the Museum of Modern Art, thank you. I made one hundred and seventy-five dollars a week, thank you. I had the respect of my parents, thank you, and the admiration of my friends, thank you, and was learning animation, thank you, and was still, at lunchtime, seeing magazines and, at night, doing illustrations, thank you. I was also miserable, thank you.

"Why do you have such a low opinion of yourself?" I was asked by Gregorio Prestopino, an artist who did freelance work for the studio. "I mean, don't you think you need help?"

Yes, Presto, I needed help. But it was not the help of somebody else I needed, except incidentally and provisionally. It was not the help of John Hubley I needed, from whom I desperately wanted to hear, "Bob, your talent is being wasted—sixty-second drop by sixty-second drop—on these foolish commercials. I want you to make a feature film for me." No, it was not his help I needed, nor could ever get, when he himself was struggling to achieve what I wanted him to hand me. Yes, I needed help, but it was not the help of my parents, who could never give me the sustaining love and warmth they did not have for themselves. Yes, I needed help, but it was not the help of Henry Wolf, or Alexander Liberman, or any editor, art director, producer, or Maecenas. They could give me all the help I needed, but it would never be enough help because it would never be the right kind of help. I know, because when I was given their kind of help—the commission for a book, the contract for a film—I didn't accept them. I was not able to see them clearly. I rejected the outstretched hands. The clock, the silently moving clock—it must be one's hour before it sounds!

In 1955 I moved away from home. That year I entered analysis (which I have never left—except technically, with the dreadful finality of my doctor's death many years later). "Courage," he would say, "is all." But courage, that is a daily fight. "Light! More light!," Goethe's cry, must precede it, but light can only be a prelude. Light allows a person to look. But only courage allows a person to see. With courage alone comes the ability to act, and the chance—the main chance, the only chance—for happiness. That year I left Storyboard, Inc.

In that year I was to take the first steps away from the unhappy known to the perhaps-happier unknown. Not perhaps-happier. Not "perhaps," children. Happier! In the very walking is happiness.

R.O.Blechman

Behind the Lines

The Fifties

My first apartment was a large, high-ceilinged studio in the Murray Hill section of Manhattan.

"Everybody who lives here becomes a success," the rental agent told me as I handed her the finder's fee, although I had found the apartment myself. "A real success!" I was to learn that my new neighbor, Leslie Saalburg, certainly was one.

Saalburg was an illustrator of the social scene. His clubby colors of maroon, mahogany brown, and pearl gray suited the always elegant ladies and gentlemen of his paintings. A dapper, mustachioed man, he might have been the model for Mr. Esky of *Esquire,* where many of his illustrations appeared. Saalburg's one-room apartment was more a drawing room than a room for drawing. It was the perfect leather-and-oak setting for the world he pictured, which was increasingly to disappear in a tumble of brick and rubble.

As my neighbor's world was to give way to a world of high-rises and finder's fees, his richly colored, lovingly detailed paintings were to be replaced by the flat stylizations of a California school of artists recently based in New York. Alongside this highly decorative illustration my minimalist drawings began to appear. Mine were less illustrations, however, than a kind of notation, a means of rendering ideas as concisely as possible with little concern for their visual aspects. (Although I was not unconcerned. I remember that I did not so much draw the cover for the magazine *Humbug* as literally paste it together. The hats that filled the skyscape were each drawn on minuscule pieces of paper which I desperately moved from place to place in search of the Platonic pattern. For hours I shifted them about until I had to give up in despair that they would ever be right. When I left the drawing table it was with dozens of the tiny things sticking to me. Days later I was still removing sombreros and stetsons from my clothing. Perhaps to other people this was a clear sign of my perfectionism. To me, in retrospect, it was as much a sign of my tentative and self-doubting nature—which might, in the final analysis, be a component of perfectionism.)

My drawings of the Fifties seem far removed from those of today. The lines were hard and characterless. My calligraphy teacher at Columbia University, where I had spent a fruitless year in 1950 studying graphic arts, viewed my brittle lines with despair. "Your line, Mr. Blechman, your *line.* Please, look at Steinberg, and see what a *line* is." I looked, but conquest of an artful line was as much beyond my means as it was outside my interests. I was, after all, a cartoonist, not an artist, and line—like form and color and composition— seemed unnecessary baggage.

My indifference to drawing showed in the way I drew eyes: the method was a variant of the cartoonist's convention of a circle with a shifting dot for an eyeball. It was to take a full decade before I realized that eyes could be rendered as simple dots, no thicker than the rest of the drawing, which were more artful than the sunnyside-up versions I rendered, and equally expressive.

Occasionally my drawings passed beyond the notative stage. In 1959 I kept a sketchbook of a four-month trip to Europe. (The trip was announced by a mailer that showed a rat escaping a treadmill, only to find himself on the endlessly spinning surface of the globe. "*Le plus que change. . . .*") The sketchbook drawings are the few of the period I can look back on without embarrassment. Perhaps because I did not have the crutches of idea and humor to rely on, they had to stand entirely on visual merit. Perhaps I felt freer in this (I thought) never-to-be published forum simply to enjoy myself and to express my innate visual sense. Whatever the reasons, this diary stands almost alone in the decade as some kind of golden metal among the dross. My neighbor, Mr. Saalburg, might have approved.

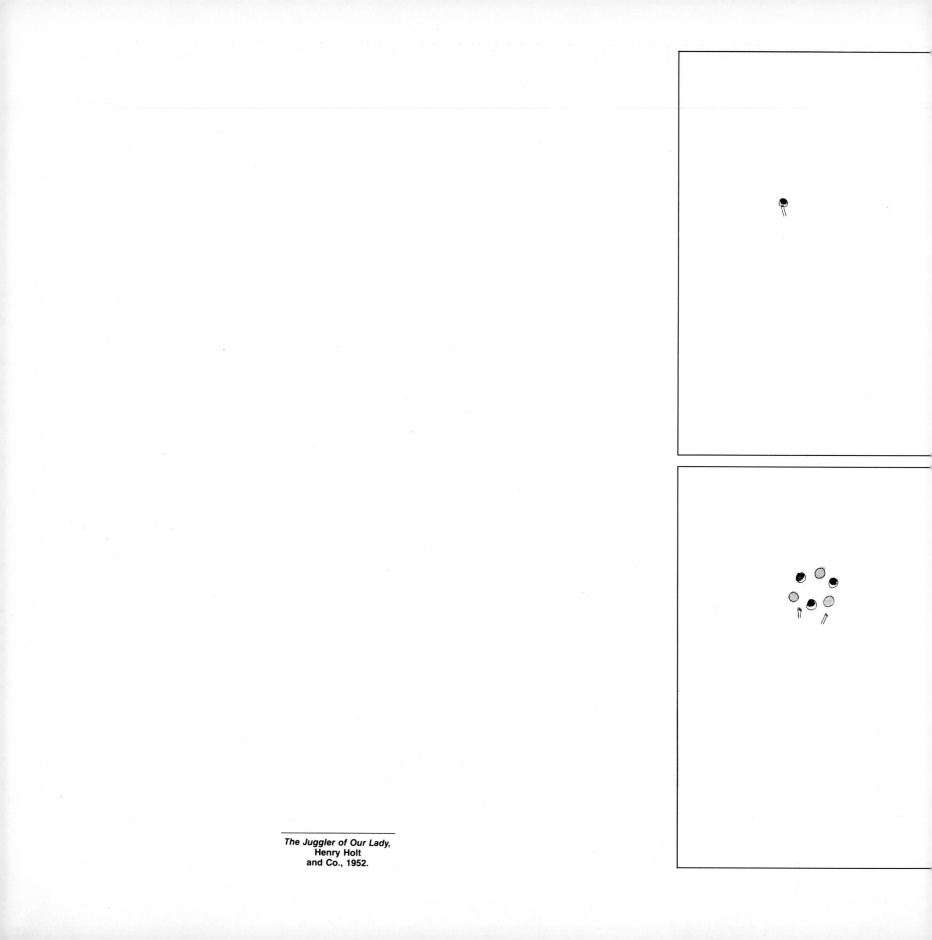

The Juggler of Our Lady,
Henry Holt
and Co., 1952.

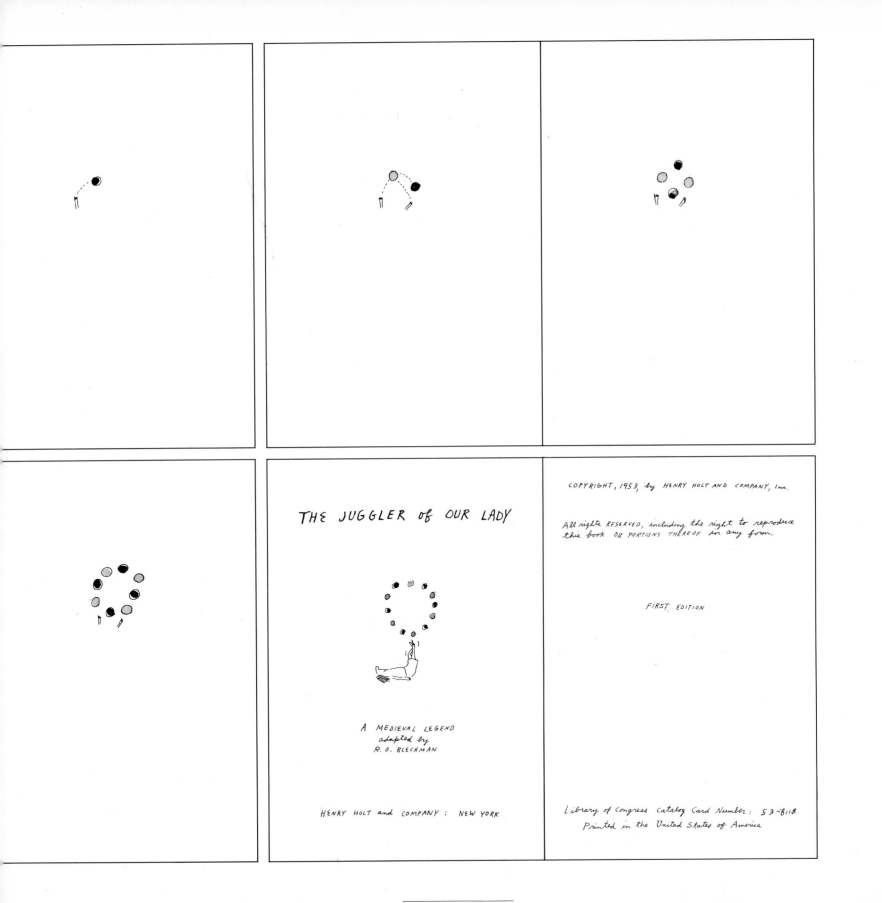

THE JUGGLER OF OUR LADY

A MEDIEVAL LEGEND
adapted by
R. O. BLECHMAN

HENRY HOLT and COMPANY : NEW YORK

FIRST EDITION

Library of Congress Catalog Card Number: 53-8118
Printed in the United States of America

A
Sort-of
CHRISTMAS
STORY

CANTALBERT WAS A Juggler.

Every morning he would walk to town with his Equipment, ...

...Unpack his DISCS, balancing CHAIR, HOOPS and BALLS, ...

... and JUGGLE.

But he could Never ATTRACT AN AUDIENCE.

He tried NEW and DIFFICULT tricks.

BUT nobody PAID ANY ATTENTION TO HIM.

But Nobody WOULD PAY ATTENTION TO HIM.

Then CANTALBERT decided that if he were m[...]
ASCETIC, Heaven would give him audien[...]
THE NEXT DAY he stood on his RIGHT HA[...]
for TWO HOURS.

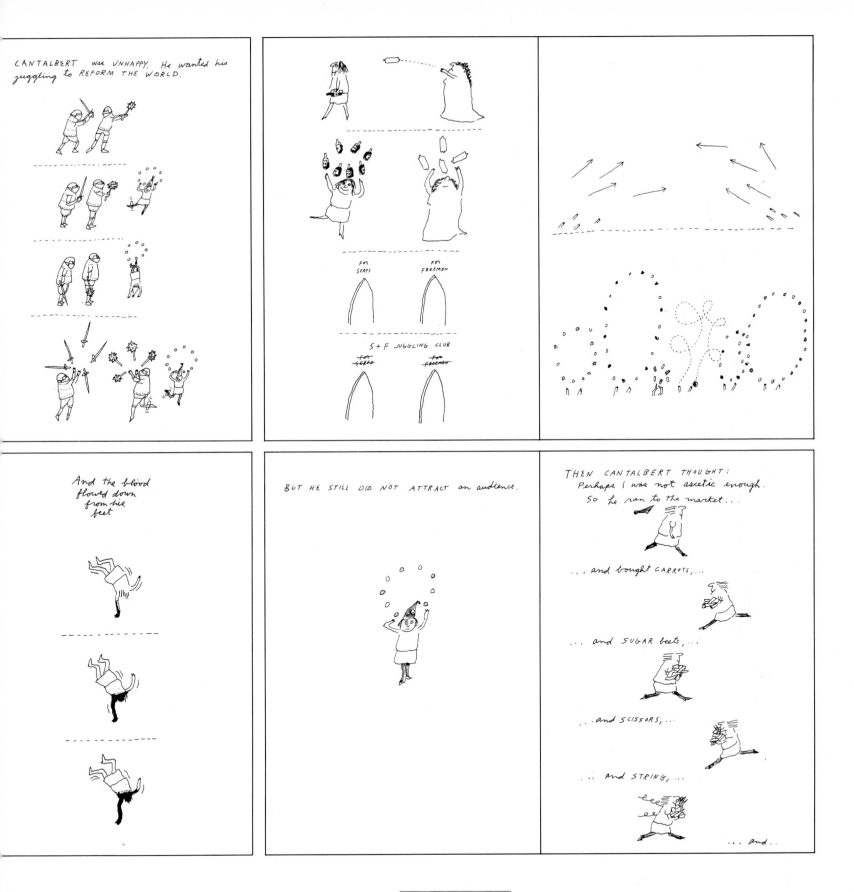

CANTALBERT was UNHAPPY. He wanted his juggling to REFORM THE WORLD.

FOR SERFS   FOR FREEMEN

S + F JUGGLING CLUB

FOR SERFS   FOR FREEMEN

And the blood flowed down from his feet

BUT HE STILL DID NOT ATTRACT an audience.

THEN CANTALBERT THOUGHT:
Perhaps I was not ascetic enough.
So he ran to the market...

... and bought CARROTS,...

... and SUGAR beets,...

...and SCISSORS,...

... and STRING,...

... and..

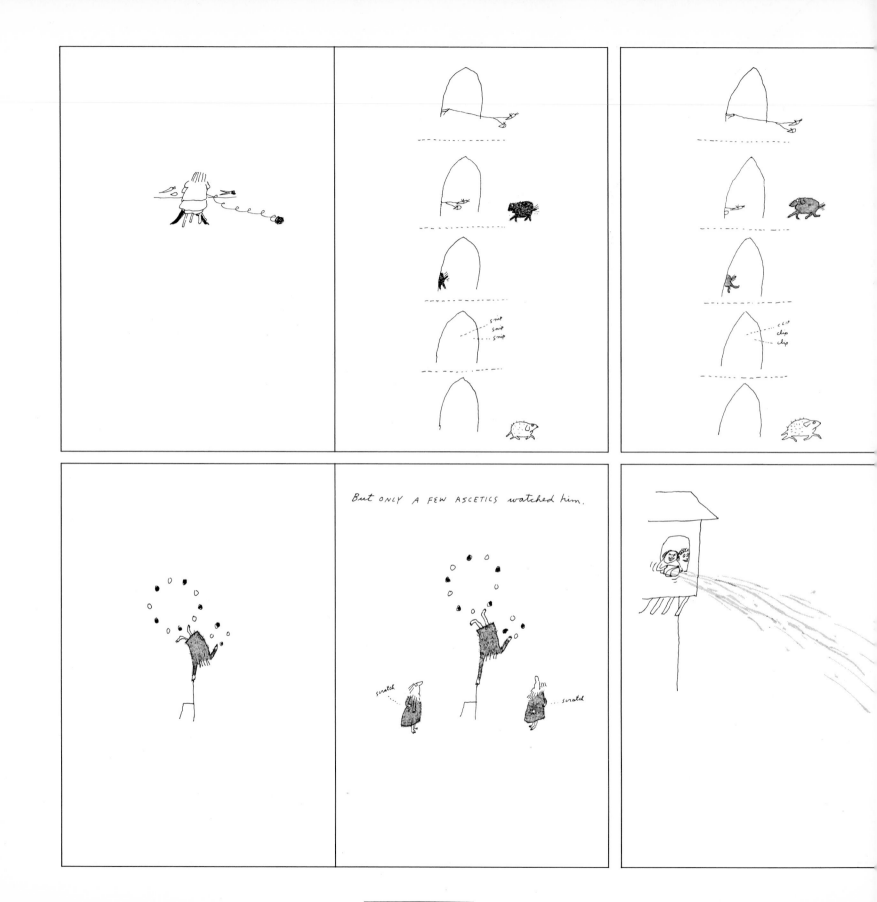

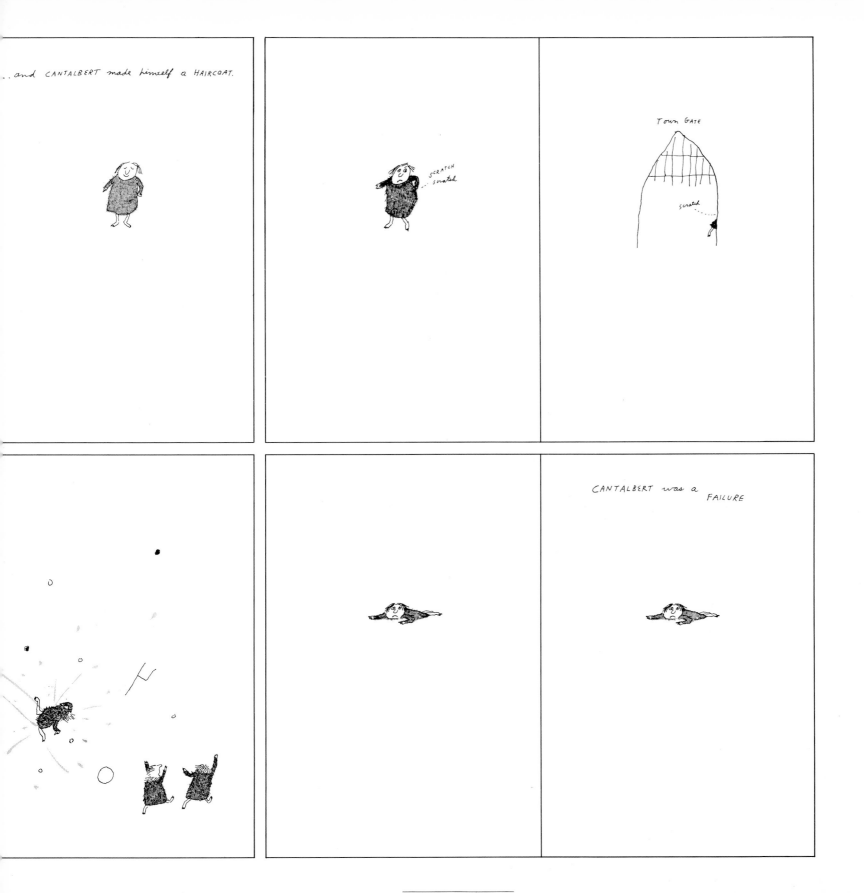

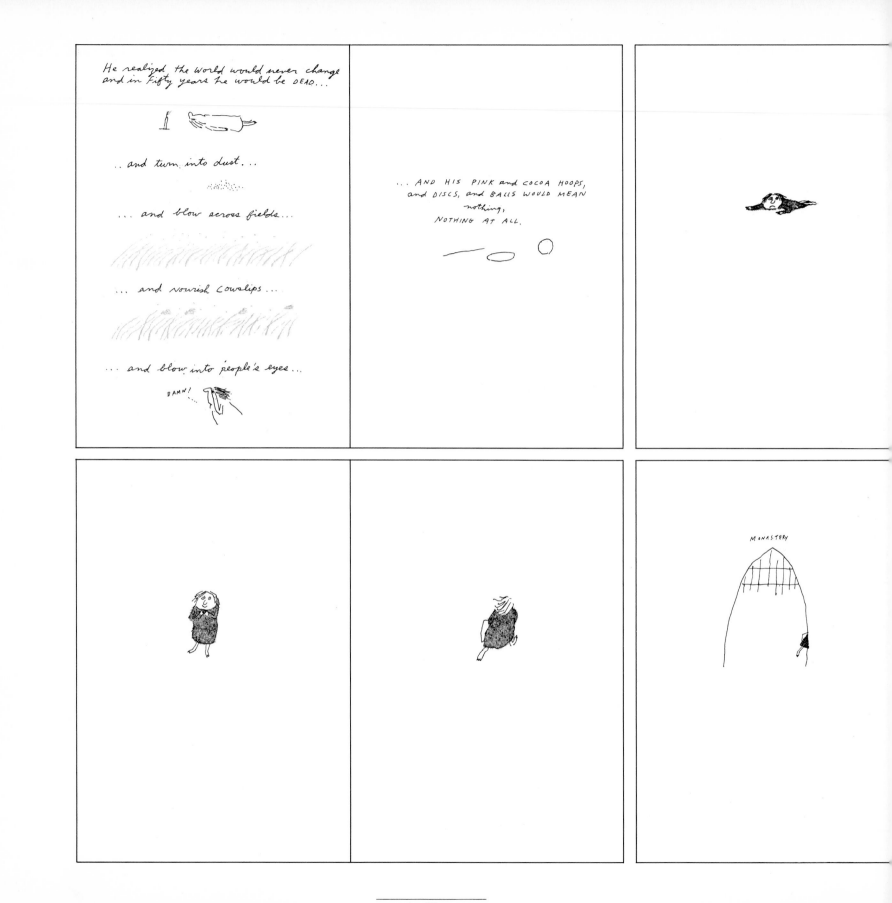

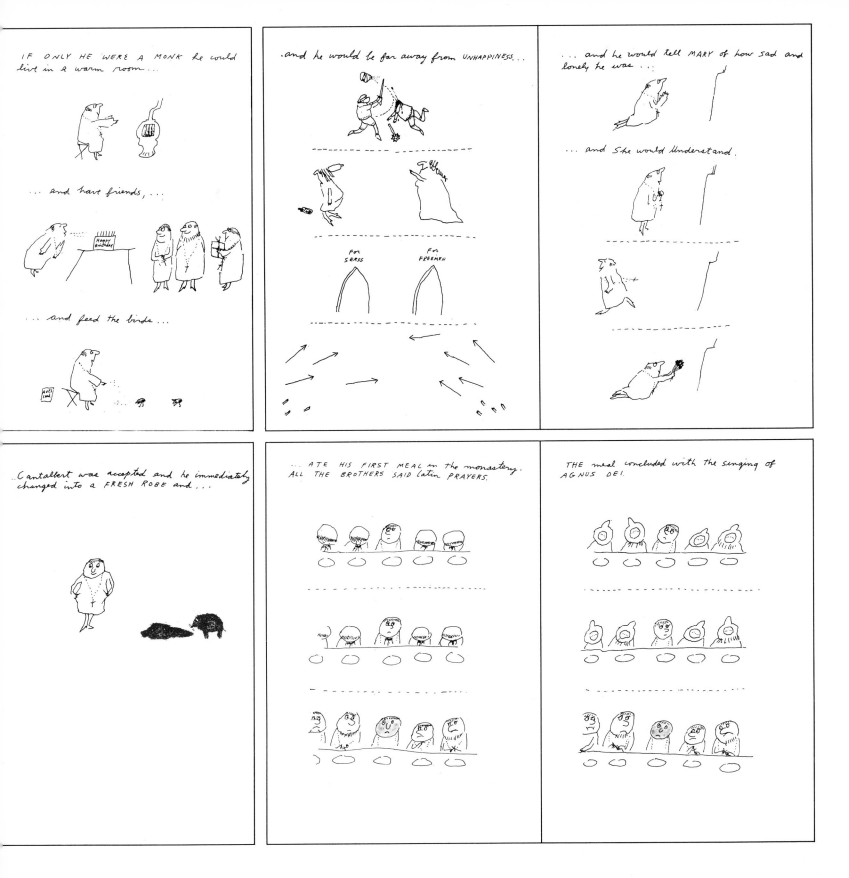

IF ONLY HE WERE A MONK he could live in a warm room...

...and have friends,...

...and feed the birds...

.and he would be far away from UNHAPPINESS...

For SERFS   For FREEMEN

...and he would tell MARY of how sad and lonely he was...

...and She would Understand.

Cantalbert was accepted and he immediately changed into a FRESH ROBE and...

...ATE HIS FIRST MEAL in the monastery. ALL THE BROTHERS SAID latin PRAYERS.

THE meal concluded with the singing of AGNUS DEI.

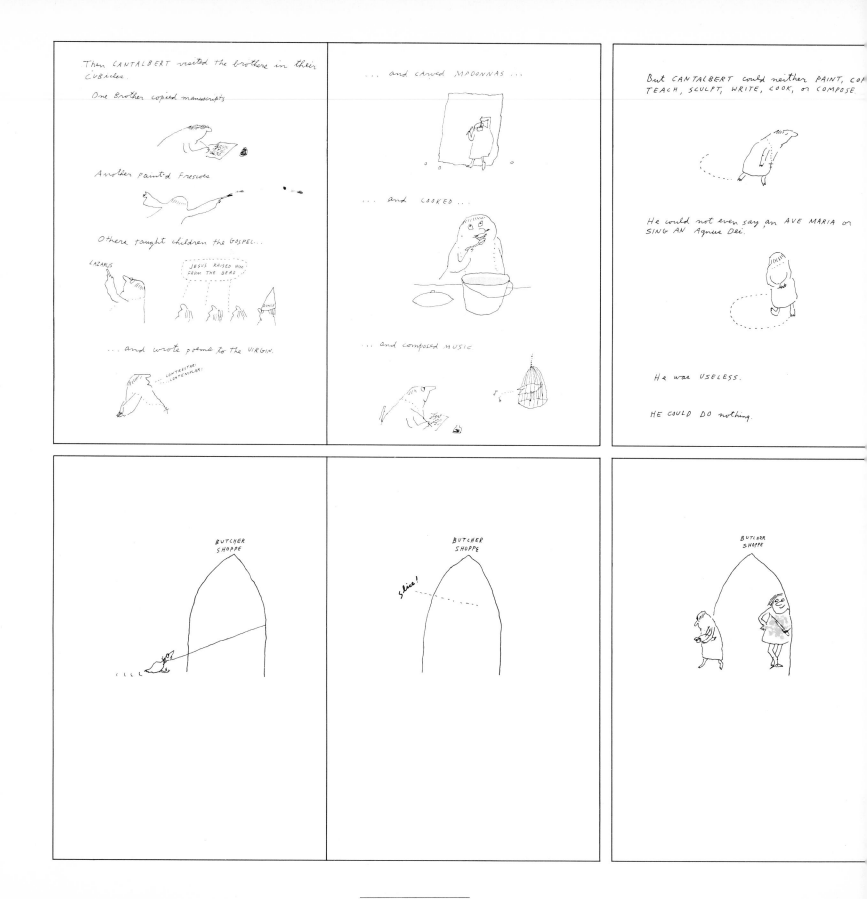

Then CANTALBERT visited the brothers in their cubicles.

One brother copied manuscripts

Another painted Frescoes

Others taught children the GOSPEL...

LAZARUS

JESUS RAISED HIM FROM THE DEAD

DUNCE

... and wrote poems to the VIRGIN.

CONTRESTARI CONTEMPLARI

... and carved MADONNAS ...

... and COOKED ...

... and composed MUSIC

But CANTALBERT could neither PAINT, COP TEACH, SCULPT, WRITE, COOK, or COMPOSE.

He could not even say an AVE MARIA or SING AN Agnus Dei.

He was USELESS.

HE COULD DO nothing.

BUTCHER SHOPPE

BUTCHER SHOPPE

slice!

BUTCHER SHOPPE

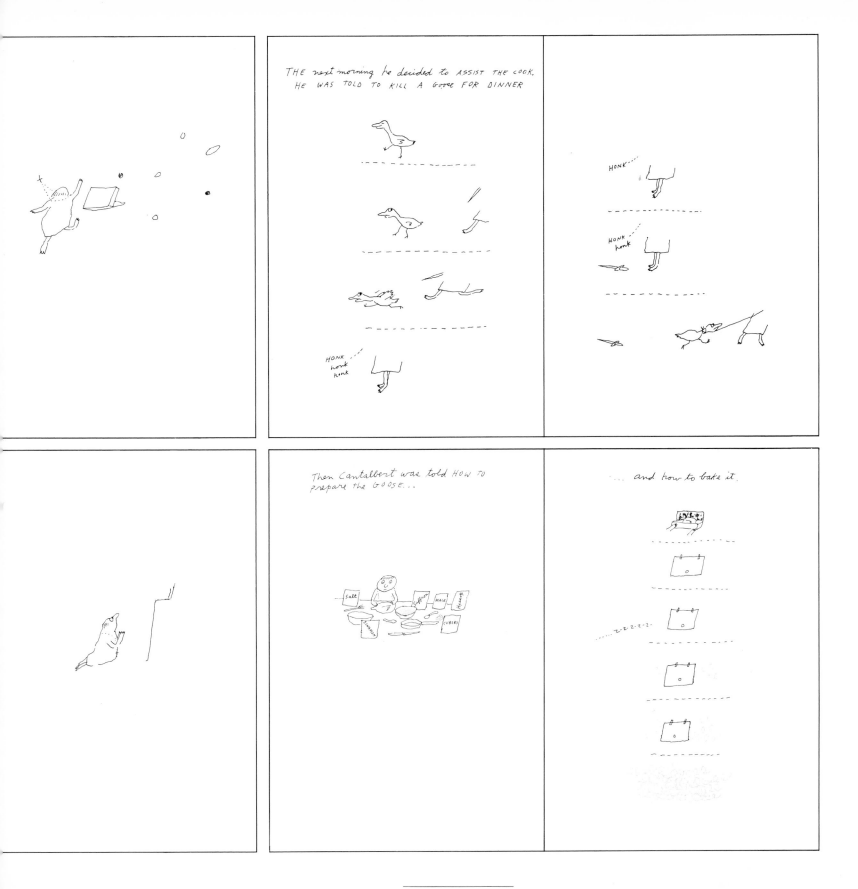

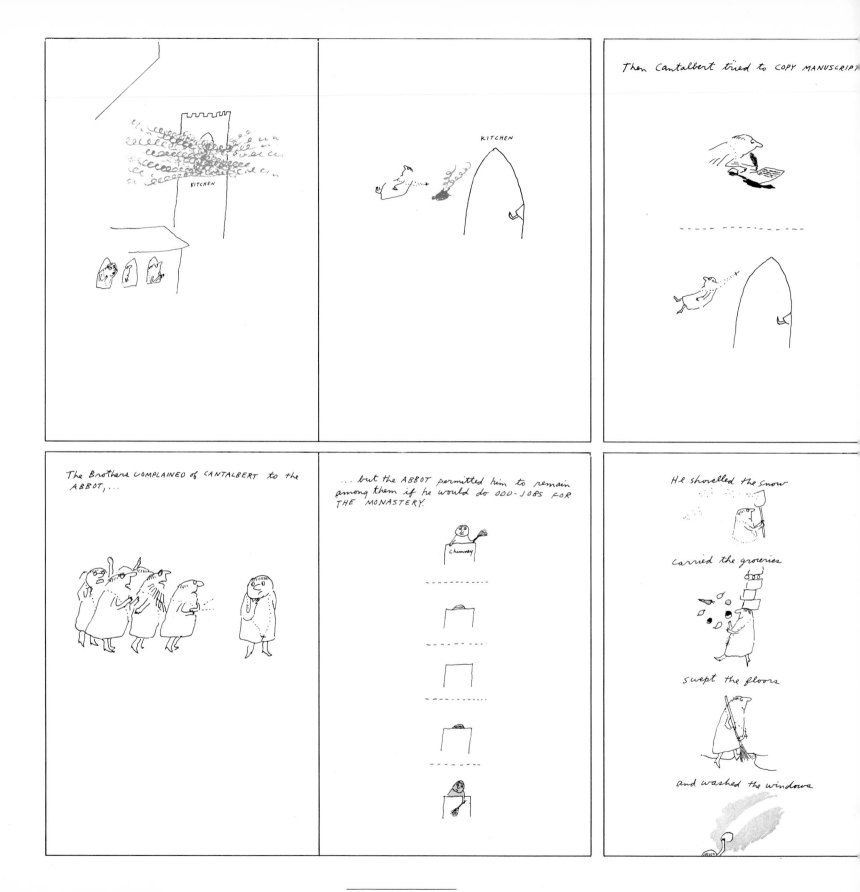

KITCHEN

KITCHEN

Then Cantalbert tried to COPY MANUSCRIPT

The Brothers COMPLAINED OF CANTALBERT to the ABBOT,...

... but the ABBOT permitted him to remain among them if he would do ODD-JOBS FOR THE MONASTERY.

Chimney

He shovelled the snow

carried the groceries

swept the floors

and washed the windows

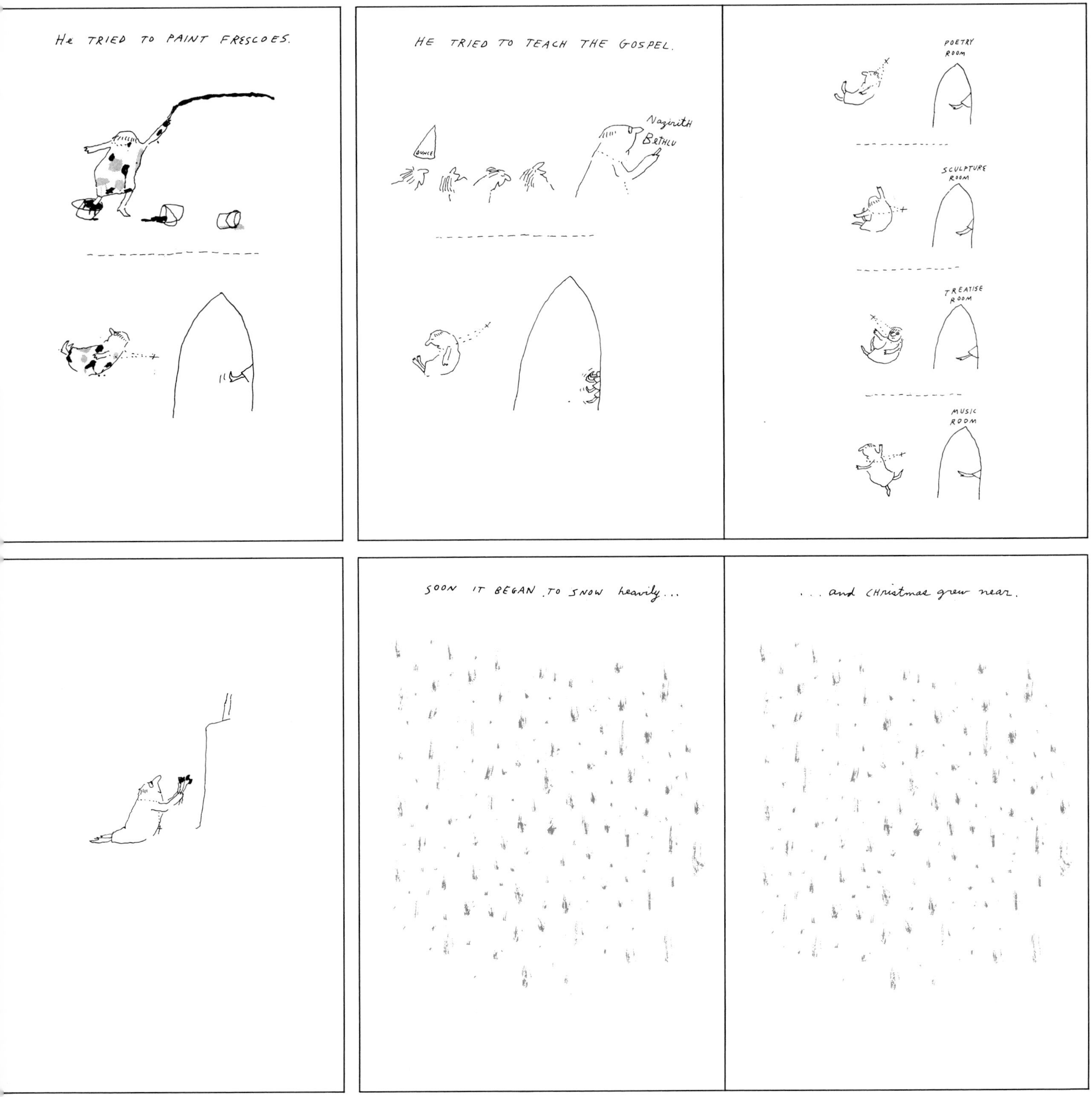

He TRIED TO PAINT FRESCOES.

HE TRIED TO TEACH THE GOSPEL.

POETRY ROOM

SCULPTURE ROOM

TREATISE ROOM

MUSIC ROOM

SOON IT BEGAN TO SNOW heavily...

...and Christmas grew near.

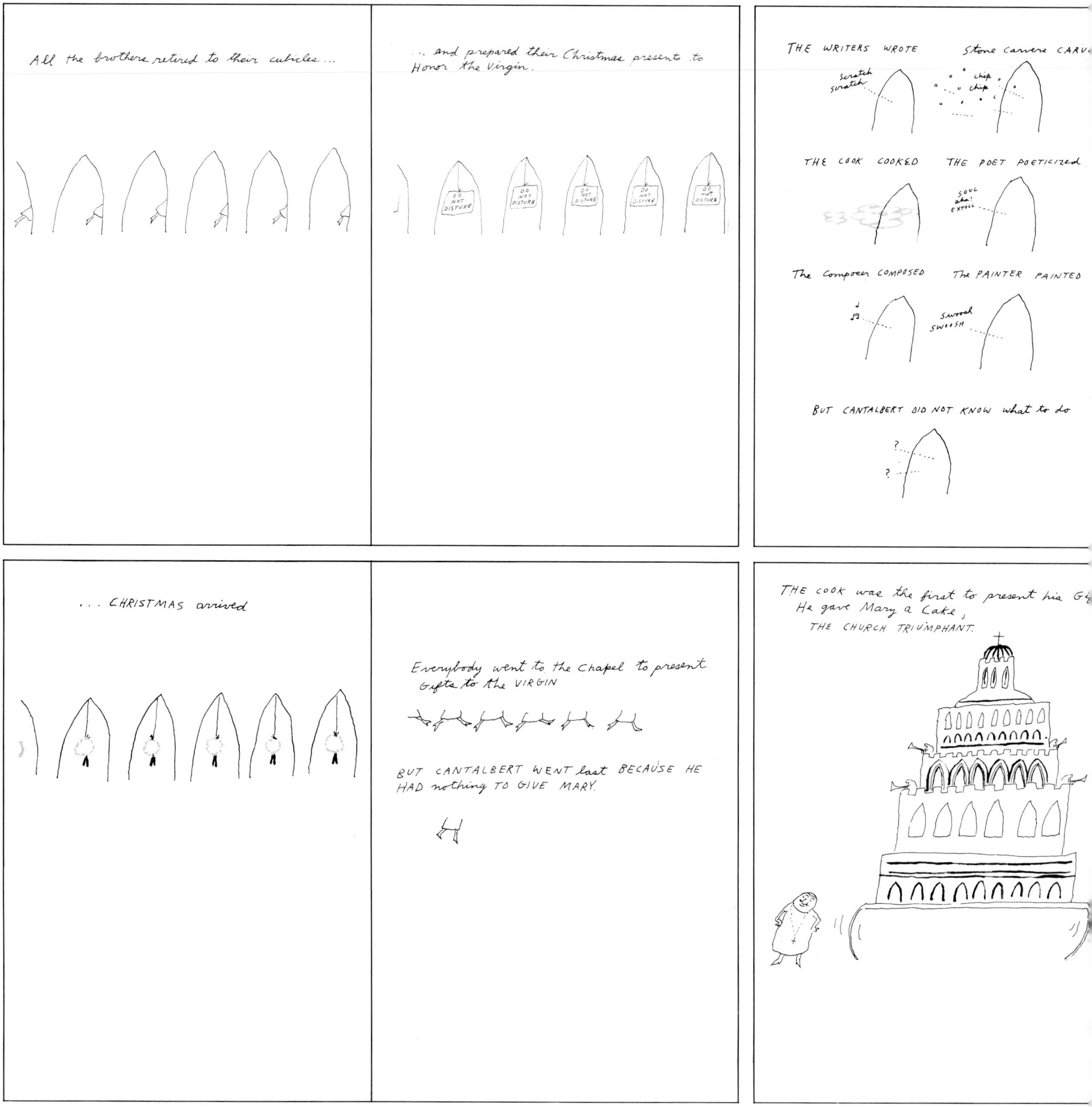

All the brothers retired to their cubicles...

... and prepared their Christmas presents to Honor the Virgin.

THE WRITERS WROTE   Stone Carvers CARVE

scratch scratch   chip chip

THE COOK COOKED   THE POET POETICIZED

83   SOUL aha! EXTOLL

The Composer COMPOSED   The PAINTER PAINTED

♫   Swoosh SWOOSH

BUT CANTALBERT DID NOT KNOW what to do

?
?

... CHRISTMAS arrived

Everybody went to the Chapel to present Gifts to the VIRGIN

BUT CANTALBERT WENT last BECAUSE HE HAD nothing TO GIVE MARY.

THE COOK was the first to present his G[...]
He gave Mary a Cake,
THE CHURCH TRIUMPHANT.

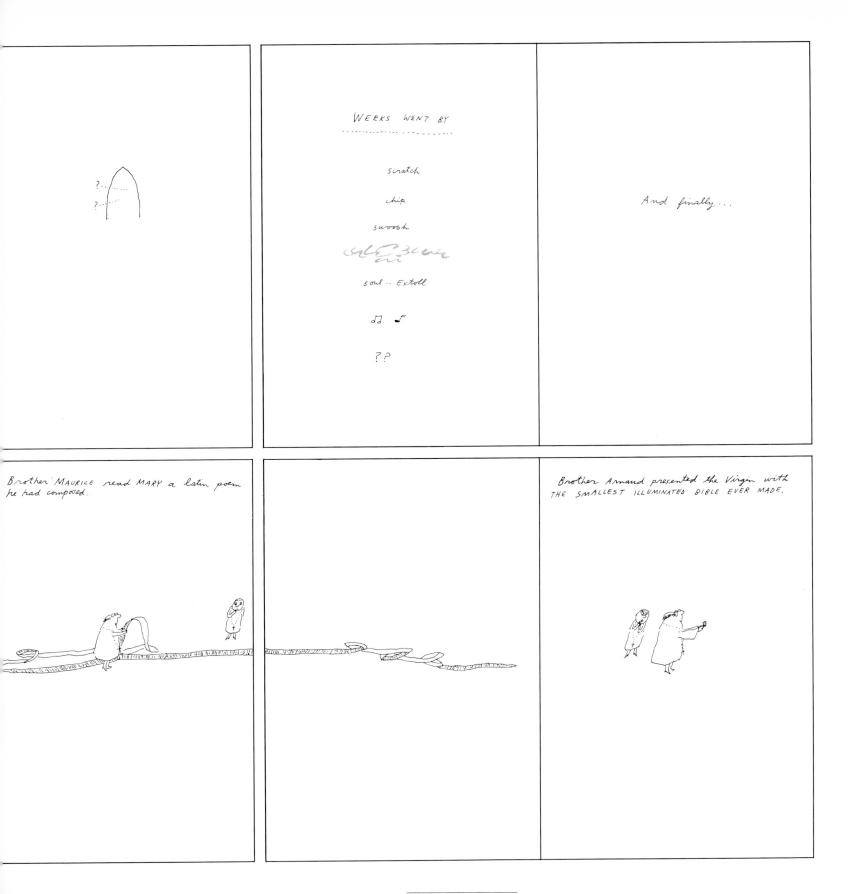

WEEKS WENT BY

scratch

chip

swoosh

soul ... Extoll

??

And finally ...

Brother MAURICE read MARY a latin poem
he had composed.

Brother Armand presented the Virgin with
THE SMALLEST ILLUMINATED BIBLE EVER MADE.

Brother Fulbert dedicated his choral
work to the VIRGIN.

Brother GUILLAME gave Mary a Triptych
of THE VIRGIN AND THE DONOR,...

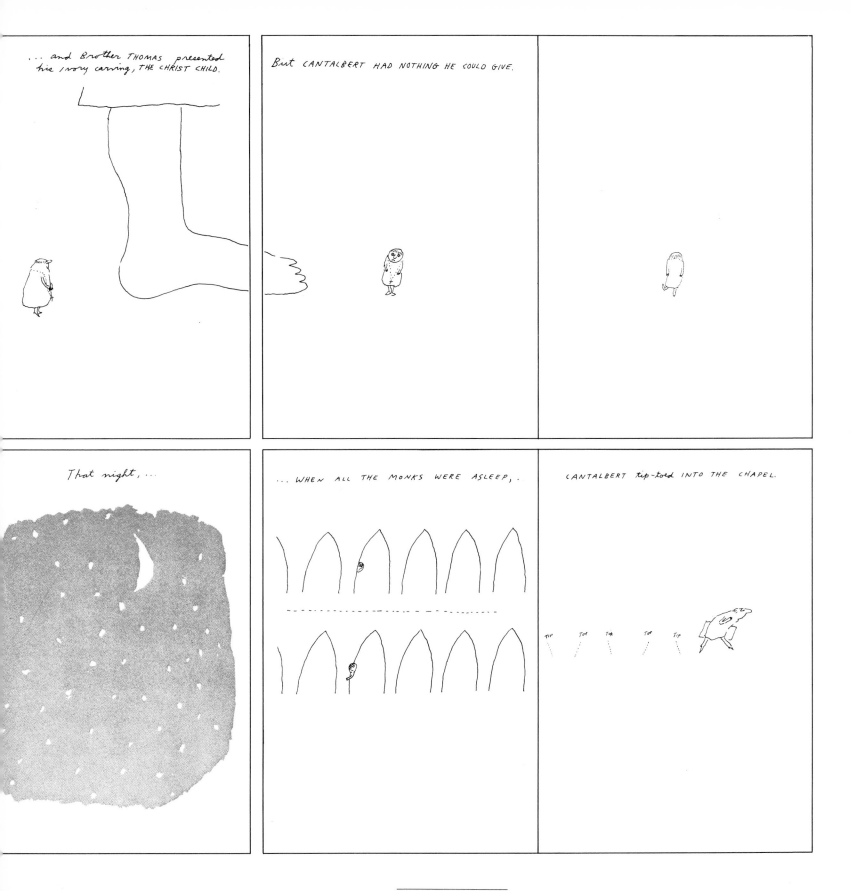

... and Brother THOMAS presented his ivory carving, THE CHRIST CHILD.

But CANTALBERT HAD NOTHING HE COULD GIVE.

That night, ...

... WHEN ALL THE MONKS WERE ASLEEP, .

CANTALBERT tip-toed INTO THE CHAPEL.

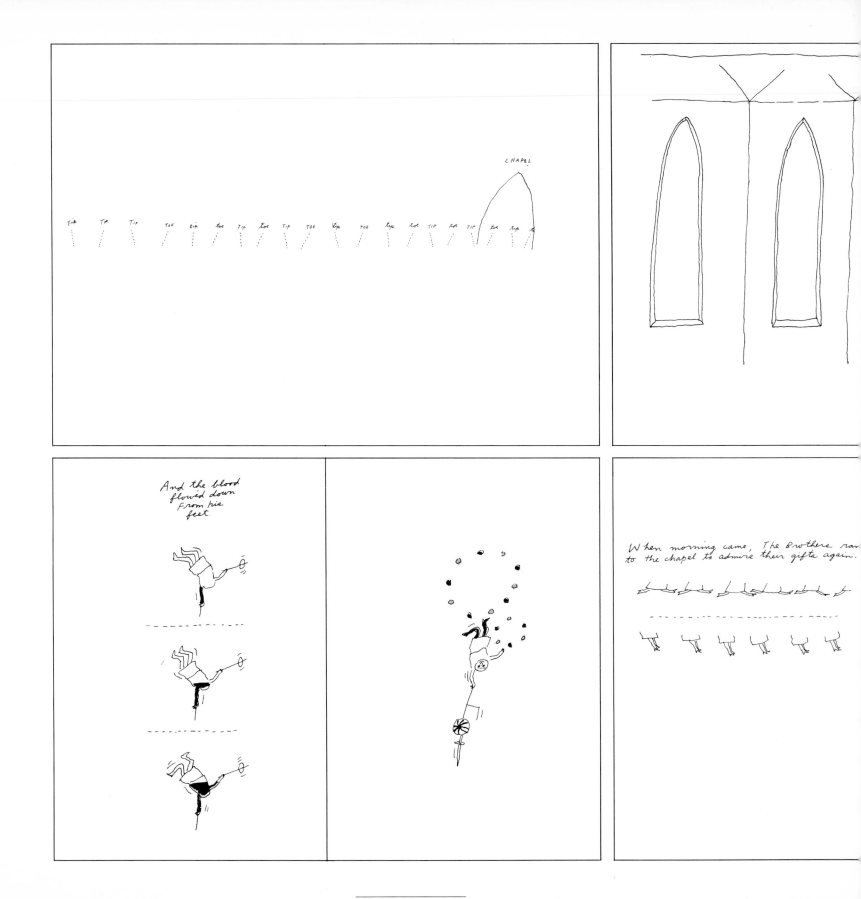

CHAPEL

Tip Toe Tip Toe Tip Toe Tip Toe Tip Toe Tip Toe Tip Toe Tip Toe Tip Toe Tip

And the blood flowed down from his feet

When morning came, The Brothers ran to the chapel to admire their gifts again.

HE JUGGLED ALL NIGHT to ENTERTAIN MARY.

Then Cantalbert collapsed from Exhaustion.

----- INSANE!

..... Sacrilege!

..... MONSTROUS!

---Desecration!

..... MAD!

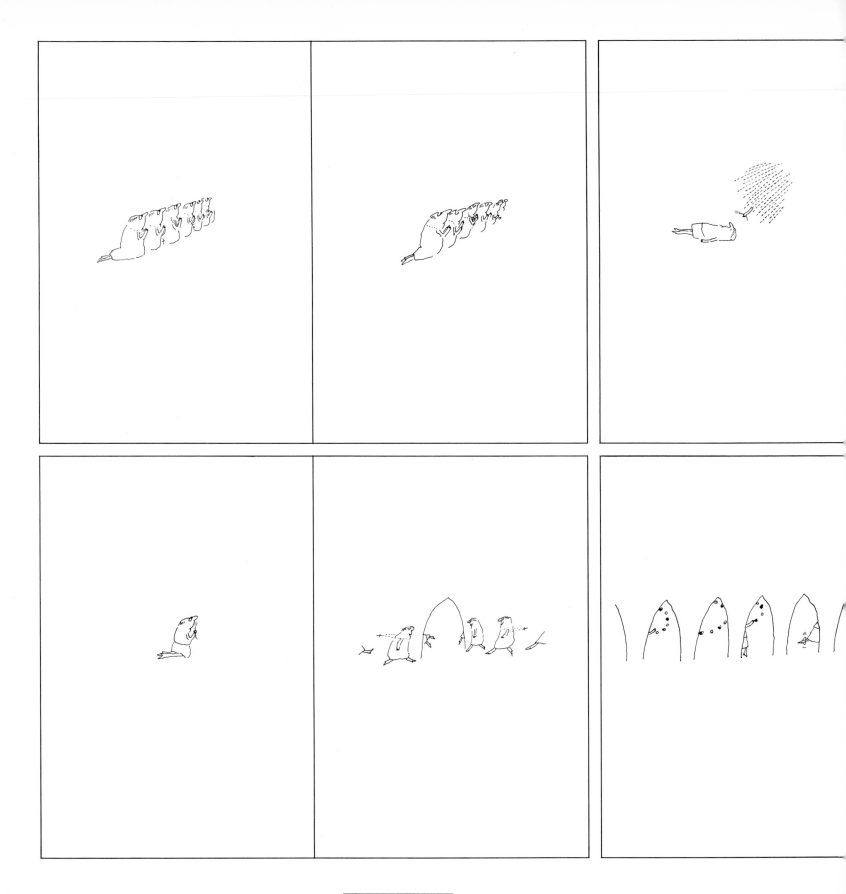

FINIS

**Illustrations
from the book *Schoolhouse*,
commenting on the
regional nature
of American schools,
Simon & Schuster, 1958.**

JOHN PAUL JONES SCHOOL

FREE
ROOF PARKING
Kiddies!

COME TO SCHOOL
AVOID PARKING
PROBLEMS

BOYS   GIRLS   VEHICLES

Detroit School

Detroit School Bus

PS 7-11
BIGGEST LITTLE SCHOOL IN THE WORLD
PS 7-11
BOYS GIRLS
NO COVER MINIMUM
TRY YOUR LUCK WIN AN A+

Reno School

ST. EMILIA SCHOOL

GOOD BOYS   GOOD GIRLS
BAD BOYS   BAD GIRLS

Gothic School
The Little Red Cloisters

PS 8 PS 8 PS 8 PS 8 PS 8 PS 8 PS 8
BOYS GIRLS LIONS FRIENDS ROMANS COUNTRY-MEN

Roman School
The Little Red Colosseum

PS 8

Greek Revival School
The Little Red Parthenon

School Chariot

Iowa School

Mississippi
Old Manse School

Old Manse
School Bus

Massachusets
School of the Seven Gables

School Bus

PS8

TODAY ONLY - MATHEMATICS
DON'T REVEAL THE SOLUTION

WYATT URP
says:
PLAY IT COOL—
GO TO SCHOOL,
PARTNER!

VISTAVISION
BLACKBOARDS

SCHOOL
IS BETTER
THAN EVER!

NEXT WEEK
The 3 R's
IN PERSON!

IMMEDIATE
SEATING!

IT'S
FUN!
IT'S
FREE!

PS8

California School

CALIFORNIA

Florida School

Georgia School

Idaho
School

May I take this Opportunity to Extend to you my Most Sincere Wishes
for a Very Merry Christmas, and my Prayers that
Health, wealth, & Happiness attend you in t

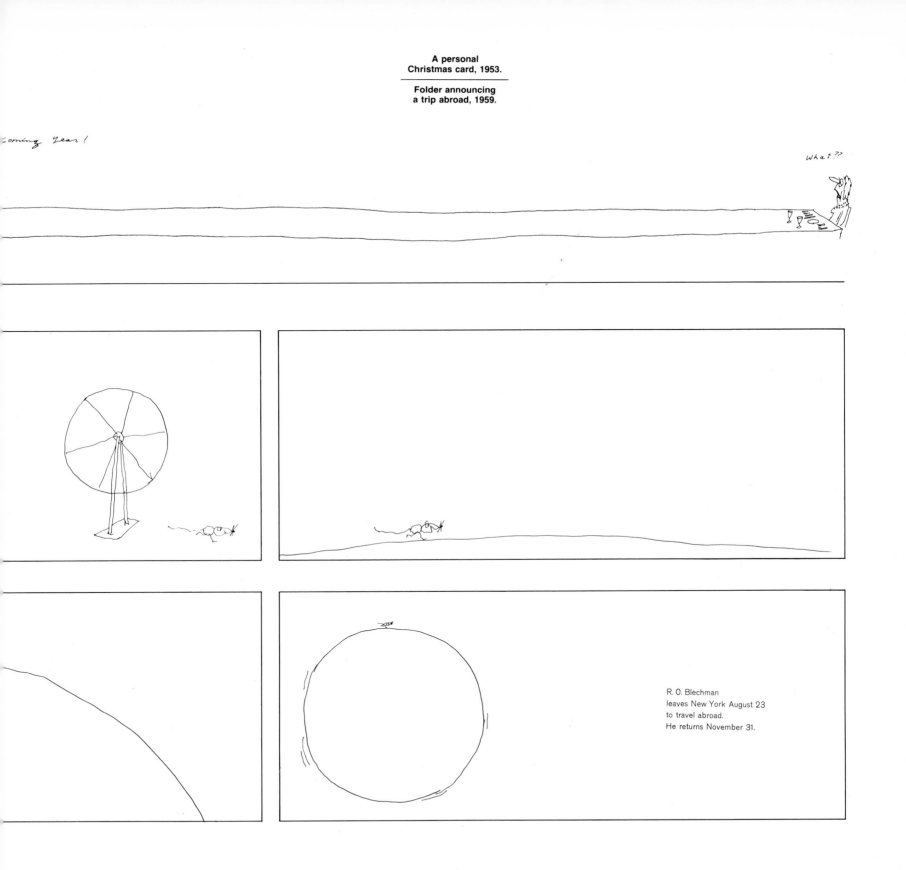

R. O. Blechman
leaves New York August 23
to travel abroad.
He returns November 31.

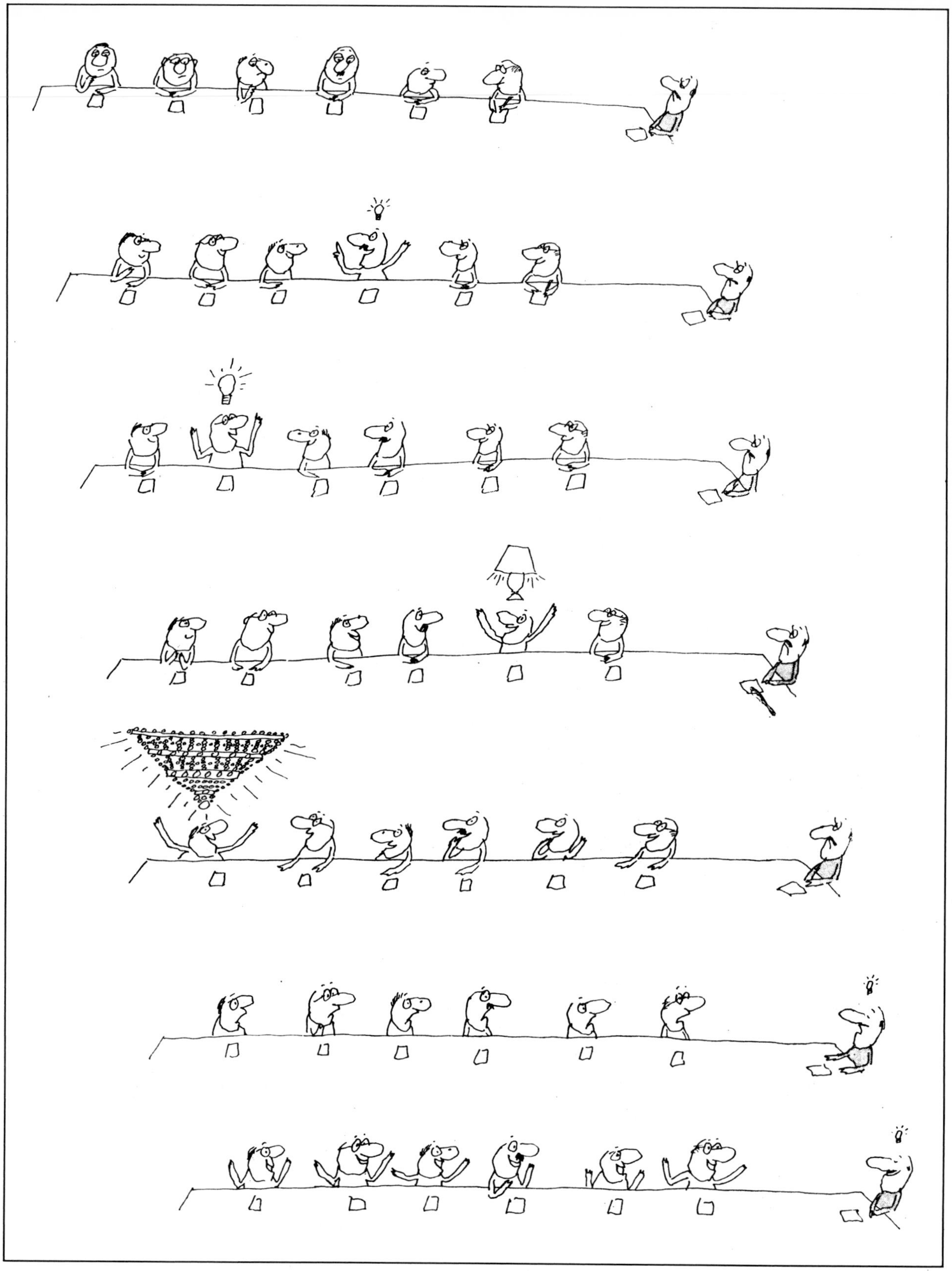

Lire it up lightly- Capezio people do! Capezio people do lire it up lightly!

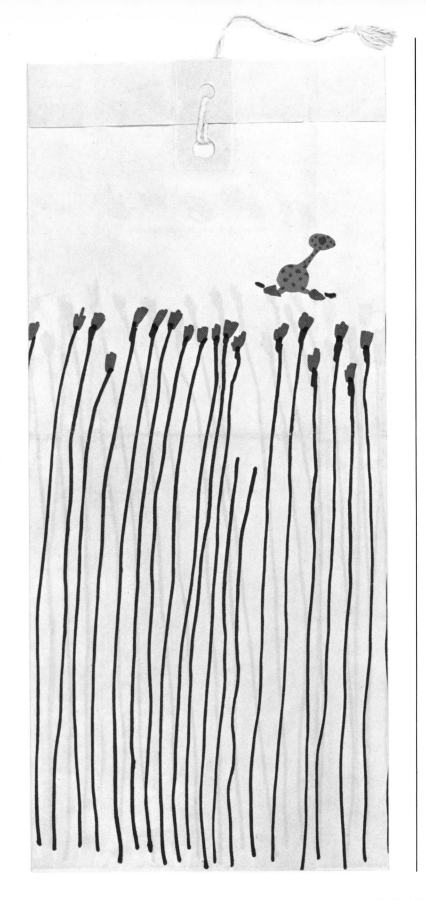

Some people can't—Capezio® people can

CAPEZIO, THE DANCER'S COBBLER SINCE 1887

MEN
BEHIND..

Living
Tape

at NTA Telestudios

...is held up by George Gould and his staff.

Last year Atlas offered the World to Mr. Gould if he & his staff would only help to carry it.

But George Gould refused, because the World does not run smoothly.

His world runs better.

MEN
BEHIND..

Living
Tape

at NTA Telestudios.

..would produce sufficient energy..

..to move the Empire State Building..

..around the World..

..Seventy Times a Second.

The Government has considered Replacing Atomic Energy with Phil's Energy

A-bomb

But Phil would rather be used for Private, Peaceful Purposes at Telestudios.

Booklets from series, "Men Behind Living Tape," NTA Telestudios, 1959.

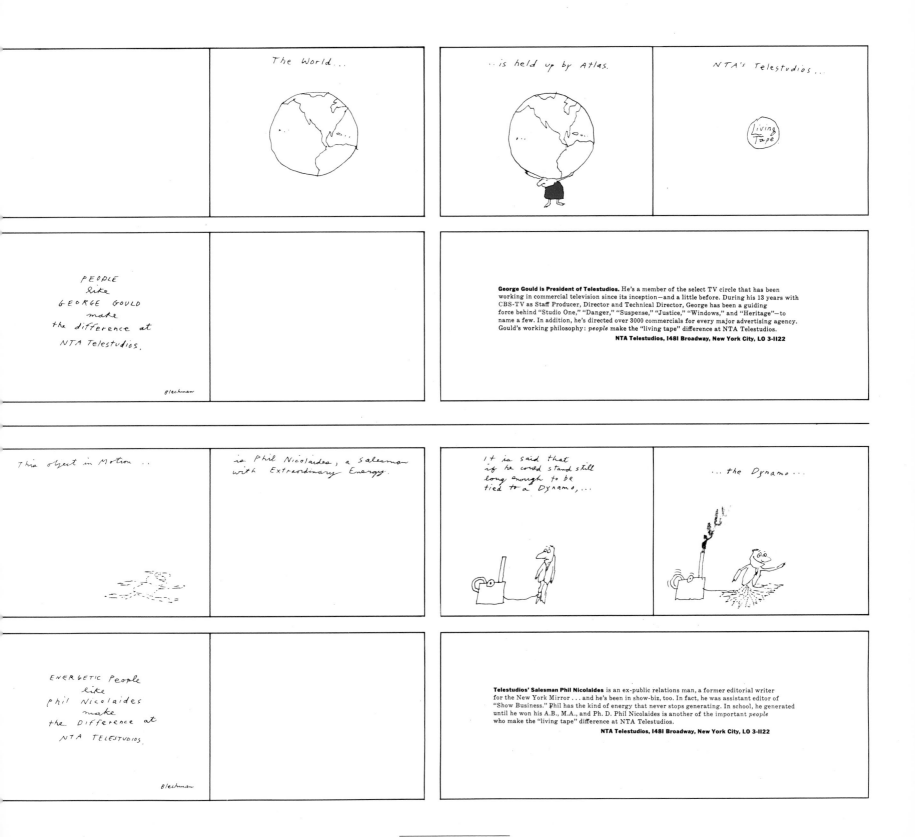

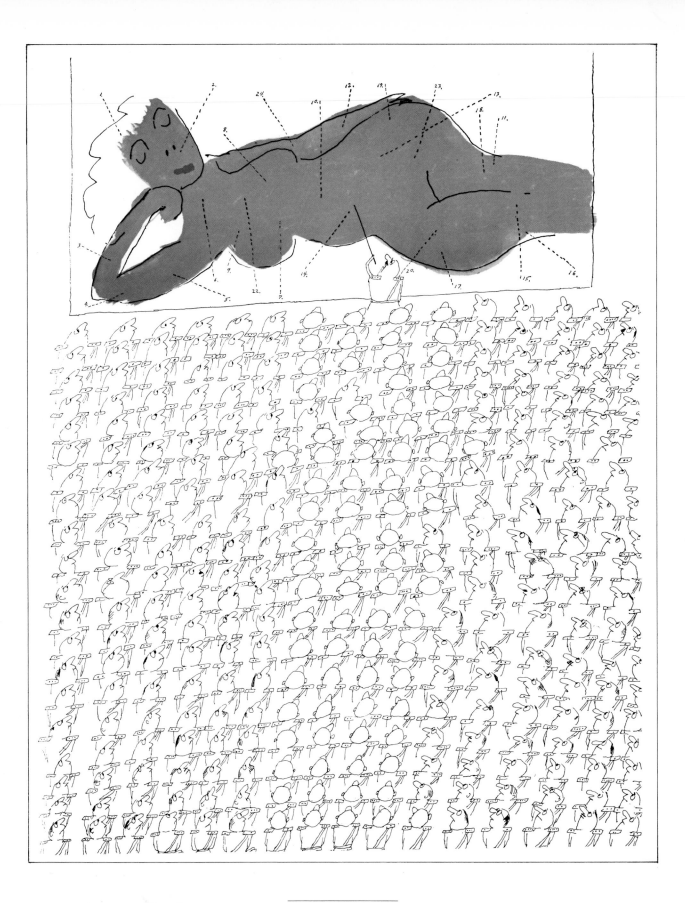

Something wonderful happens when you wear "Intoxication" by

D'ORSAY

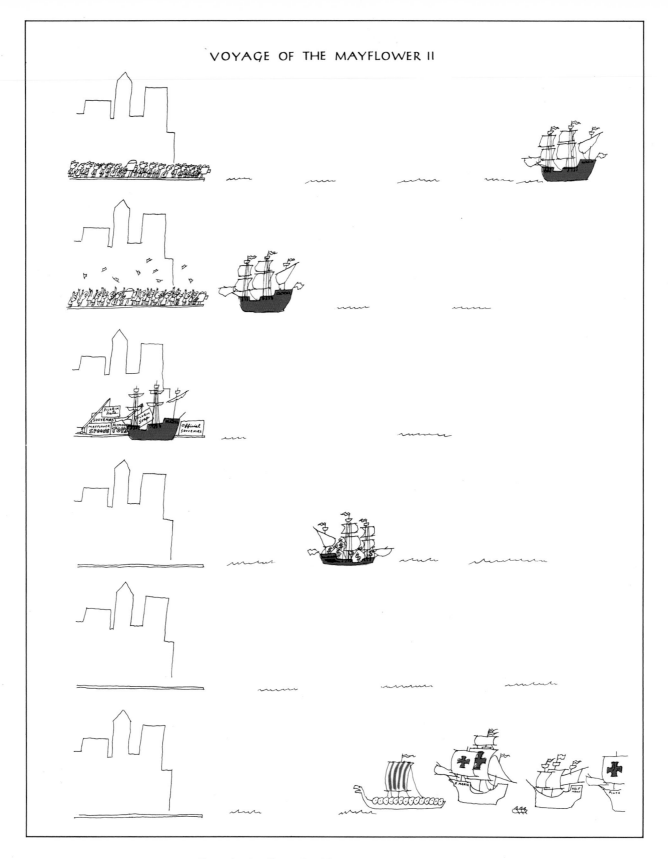

Promotional mailer reprinted from *Humbug* magazine, 1957.

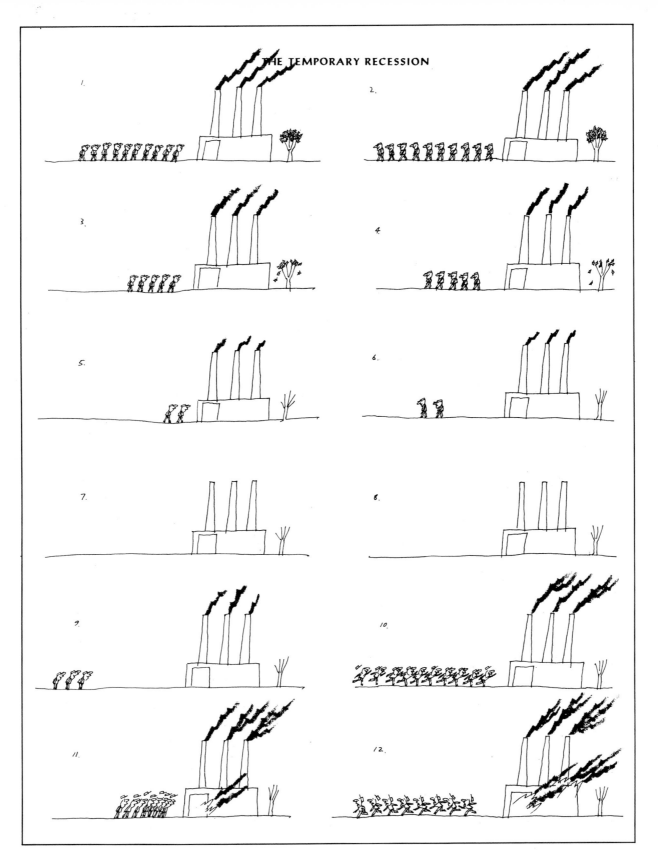

Cartoon, *Trump* magazine, 1956.

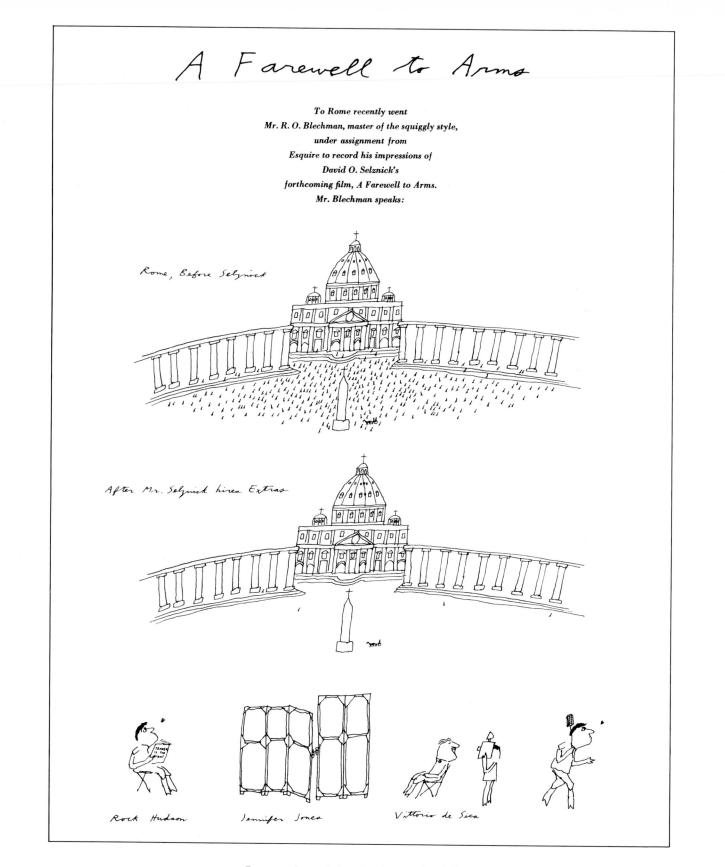

A Farewell to Arms

*To Rome recently went
Mr. R. O. Blechman, master of the squiggly style,
under assignment from
Esquire to record his impressions of
David O. Selznick's
forthcoming film, A Farewell to Arms.
Mr. Blechman speaks:*

Rome, Before Selznick

After Mr. Selznick hires Extras

Rock Hudson

Jennifer Jones

Vittorio de Sica

Two pages from a feature, *Esquire* magazine, 1957.

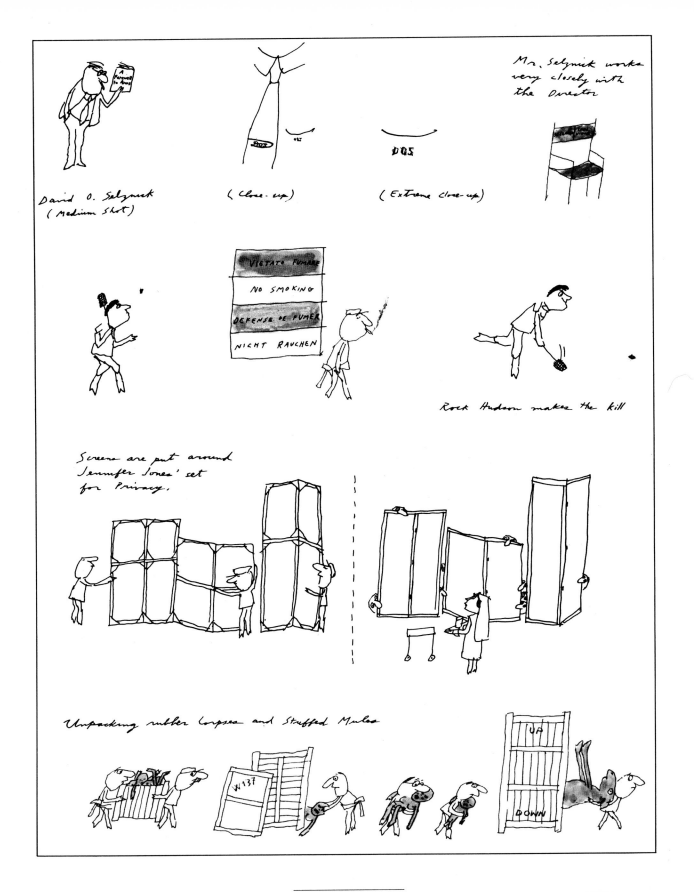

Aug. 23

The band played "Anchors aweigh" & the boat started to move & Moisha started to cry, & then the band began "Auld Lang Syne" & my parents & friends & in-laws grew smaller & I began to cry

Hercules was in his cabin most of the day suffering from a toothache. The ship's doctor cannot extract it. He must wait to Naples.

We visited the Tourist class section. There were no lights on their outside decks & no footrests in the few chairs they had. No wonder the TC passengers pause at the pool as they go to the 4PM chapel service.

When you press a button

a dull light outside of your cabin & a second one on the corridor.

Tomorrow we are waking up at 6 AM (Moisha has set her mental alarm clock) to watch our boat entering Naples Harbor.

Asked Domenico to awaken us.

Sept. 3

A bad night. When I finally fell asleep I dreamt I was still awake. At 5:15 I woke up & saw that it was light. "Moisha" I cried "The sun is up." But the sun had just begun its rise, just like us. I climbed up the ladder to Moisha's berth to see out of the port hole.

"Land!"

We dressed & Moisha quickly put on her makeup & 15 minutes later we were on deck. The sailors were washing the deck down with hose & brush. Seven older pass's were entering chapel.

It was windy & M had to return for a cedar

"Welcome"

Horse & cart for luggage

Nouveau-Riche Greek-Americans

Port: Lebanese boat unloading (cedar?) Lumber

Customs Office & the "Tampax incident"

Pages from a diary of my European trip, 1959.

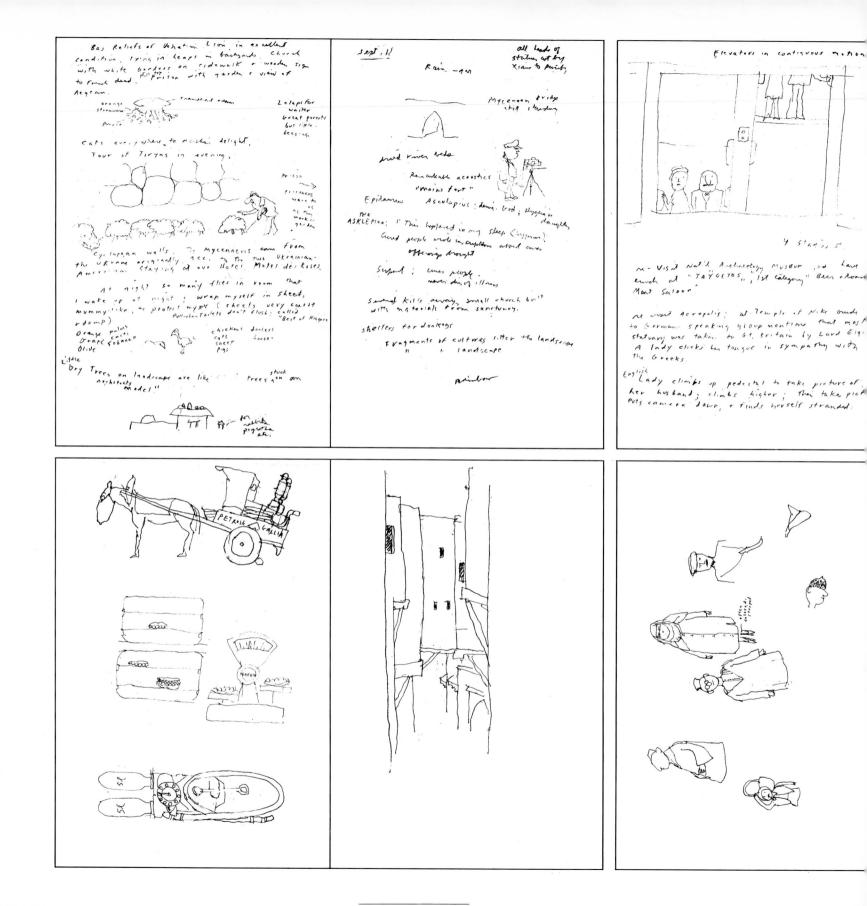

Thanksgiving at the Gordons
with the Turkey watching us
prepare his stuffing

Sometimes he felt guilty about his work.

It was his job to play with the other sheep, and then lead them to the slaughterhouse.

The Sixties

My studio was no longer at home. I shared space with a designer named Tony Palladino, and as the design firm of Blechman & Palladino we set out to grid the world crisply in the Swiss manner. The firm lasted a brief and splendid year, breaking up I suppose on the shoals of ego, although I never did learn the exact reason for my partner's abrupt departure. I set up for myself, returning to my primary field of illustration, but continuing to dabble in design.

On East Forty-eighth Street I found a penthouse studio with a skylight straight out of *La Bohème*. It was a modest five-story walkup, but beyond my roof deck lay the world. Or more precisely, Madison Avenue, which was to become increasingly my world. Although Madison Avenue was to ensure that this Rodolfo did not have struggles with finances, the moral struggles were considerable. It was 1962, and Schwerin, Chaney, and Goodman were setting out from their comfortable northern homes for the racial wasteland of the South. Sometime before their battered and swamp-logged bodies were found, my ads appeared for the state of South Carolina where, the tag line proclaimed, "You can start operating in the black faster."

I operated very well in the black myself, but not without real discomfort at the Mephistophelean swap to which I felt I had agreed. I was to exercise more social awareness with some of my clients in the future. But it was hard to determine which commissions to accept and which to refuse. Where was my pen, avowedly for hire, to draw the moral line?

I knew it had to be drawn somewhere. I chose not to advertise cigarettes, promote Muzak, illustrate *Playboy,* or do a commercial for Coca-Cola when the agency seemed to target the project for Coke addicts. But between these black and white poles lay a vast gray (and green!) world of commissions, and I did not know how to chart my course.

Occasionally I escaped the moral dilemmas of commercial art by doing editorial art, but these ventures were few and infrequent. When my book *Onion Soup* came out in 1964, it met with a smattering of reviews and sluggish sales. I was so discouraged that I did not write another book until a decade later. When the *Village Voice* published my Vietnam cartoons, their readers' lack of response ensured that these cartoons would be followed by no others. I would have happily suffered naysayers, but the burden of silence was insufferable, and my fragile spirit broke.

During the Sixties, other artists of my generation exploded in new visual directions. I imploded, concentrating my pent-up emotion and visions in the occasional drawing or story that became a distillation of my thought and feelings, a haiku *War and Peace.* A friend once said to me, "Bob, concentrate on shorter pieces. They are your forte." My friend was right, I am sure. But right for the person I was, not for the person I was determined to become.

Three stories
from *Onion Soup and
Other Fables*,
The Odyssey Press, 1964.

1. "Onion Soup"

MORAL: Too many broths spoil the cook.

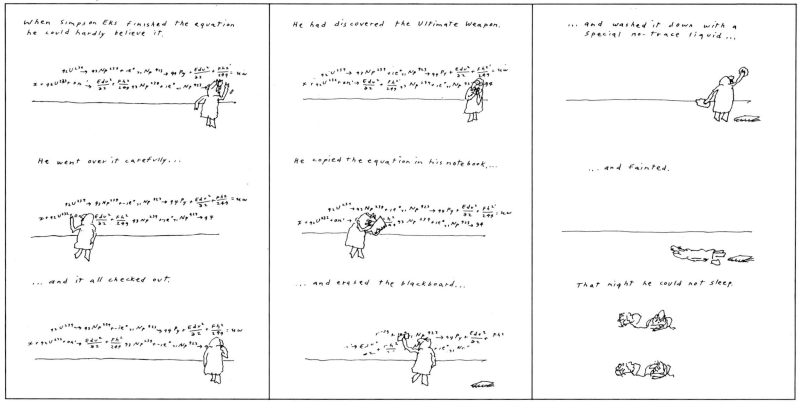

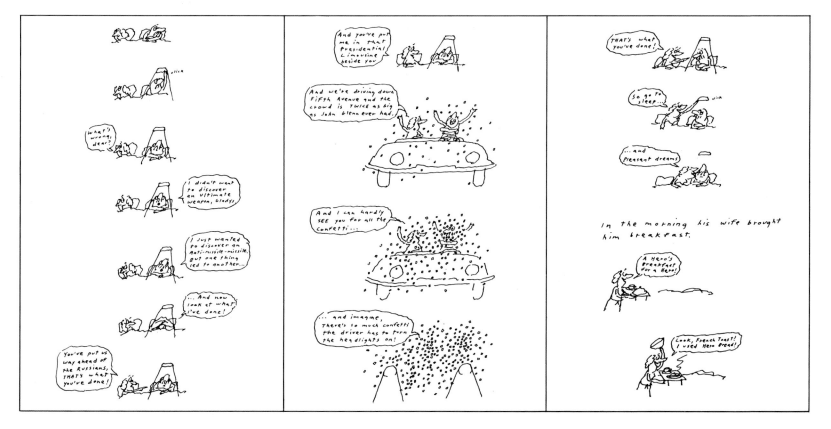

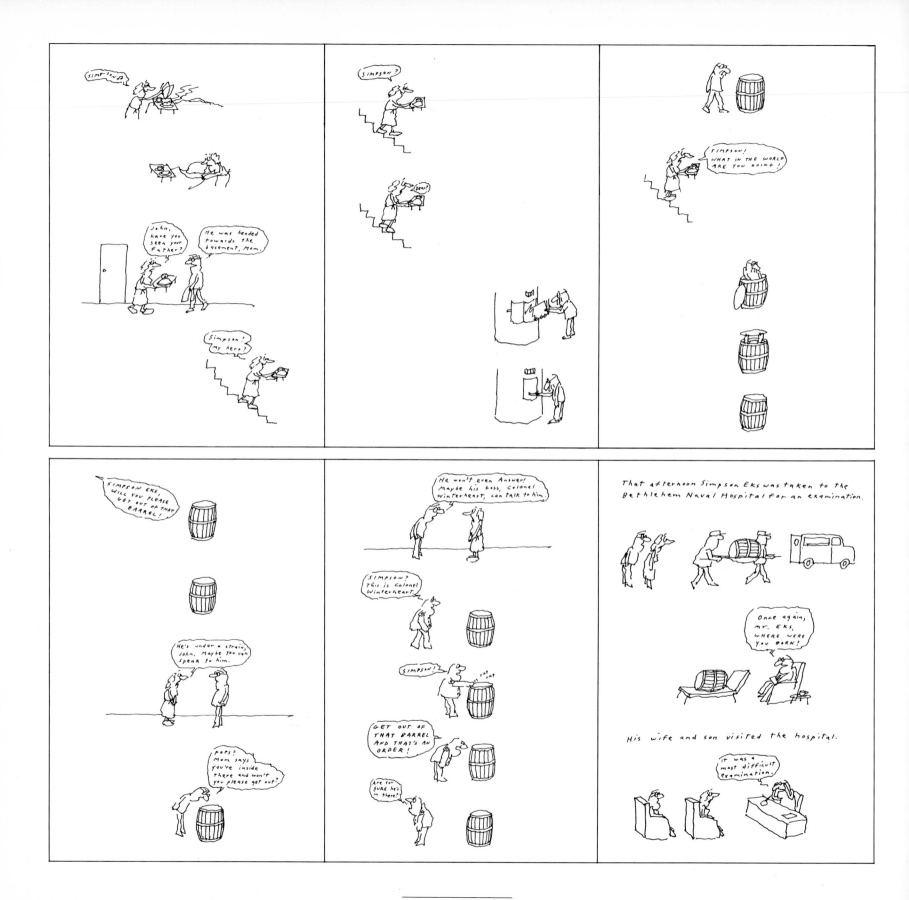

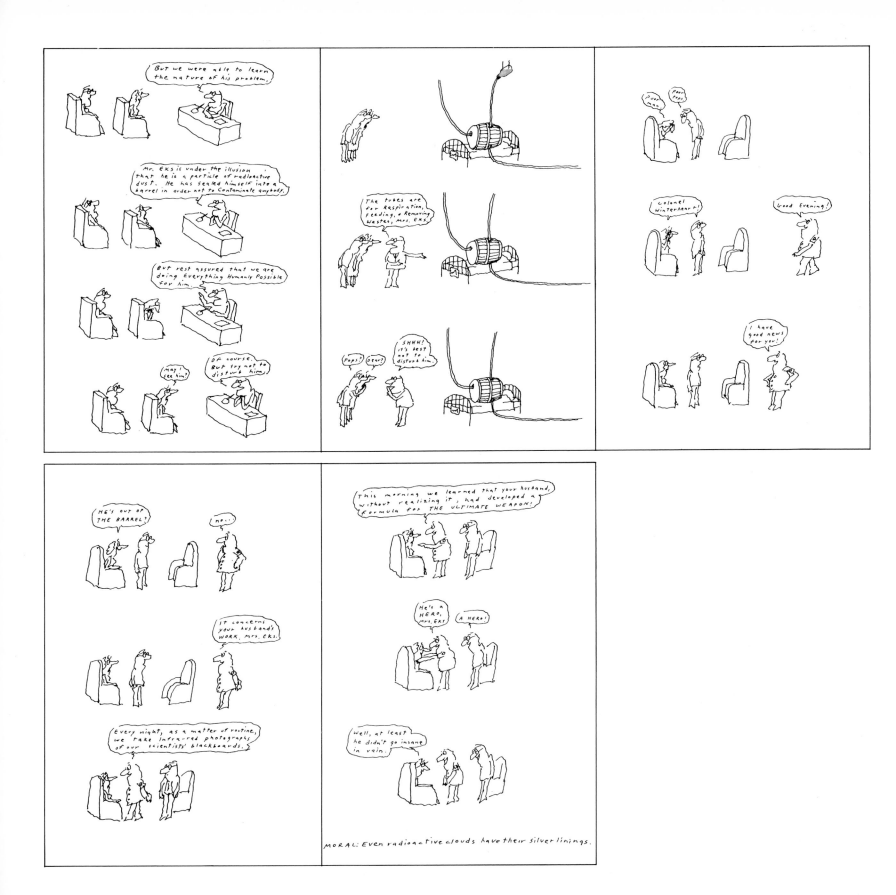

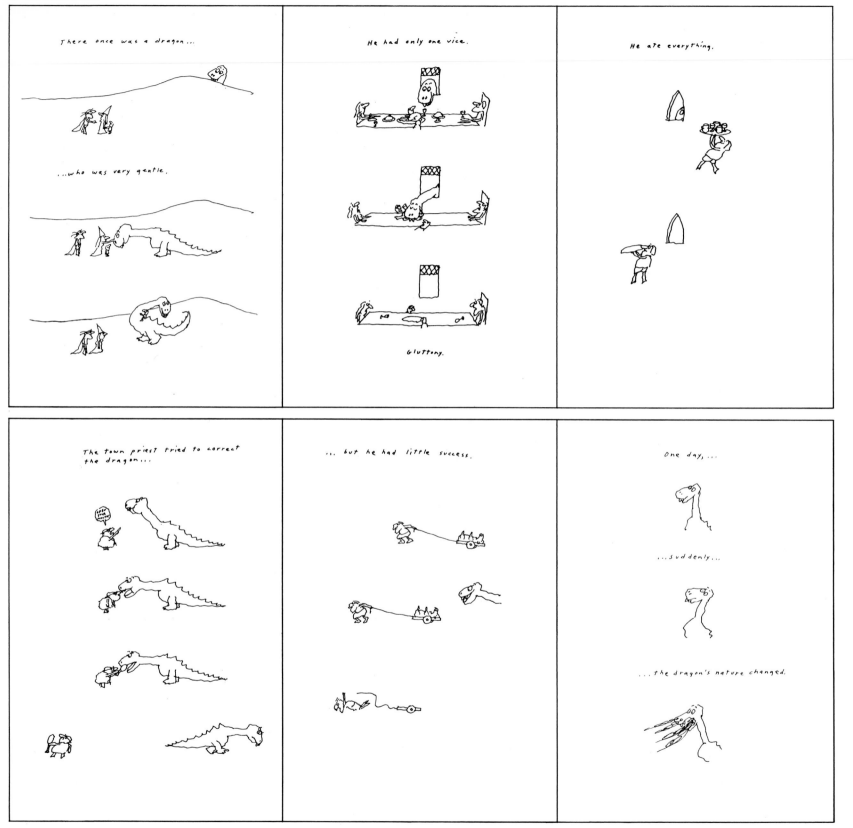

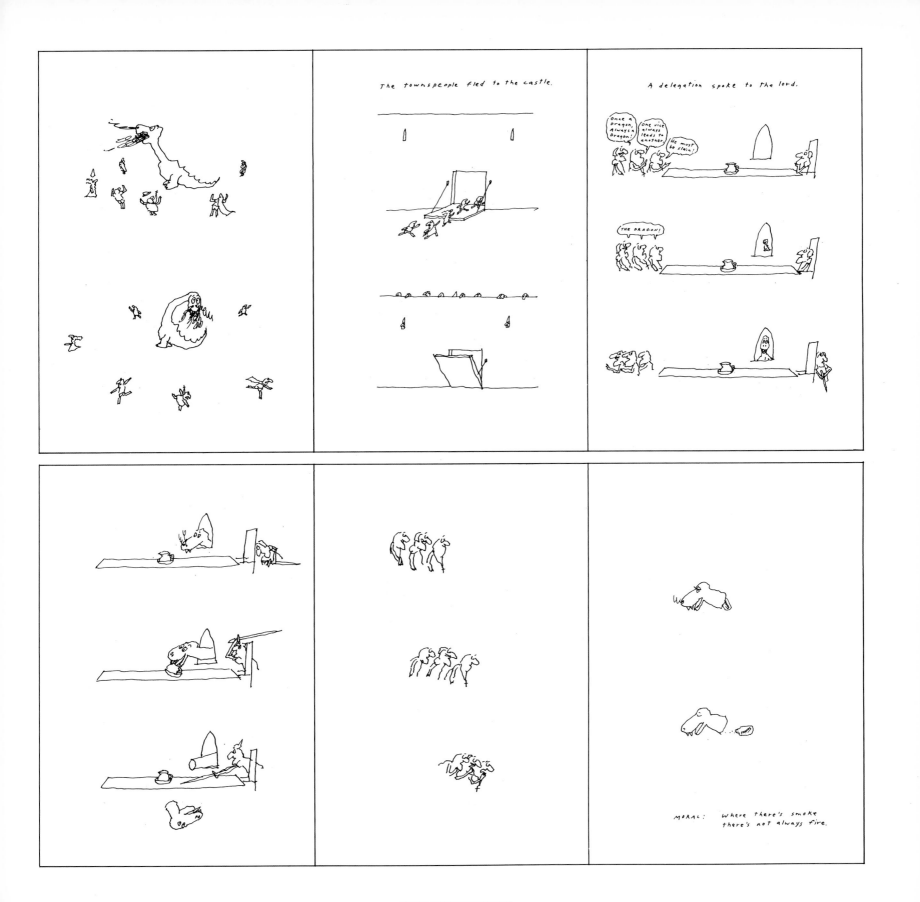

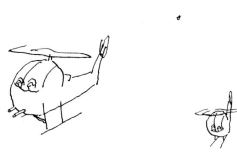

Editorial cartoons
on the Vietnam War,
Village Voice,
1965, 1966.

Illustration for
"She's a Woman,"
*The Beatles
Illustrated Lyrics*, 1969.

Valentine's Day page,
Esquire magazine, 1961 [right].

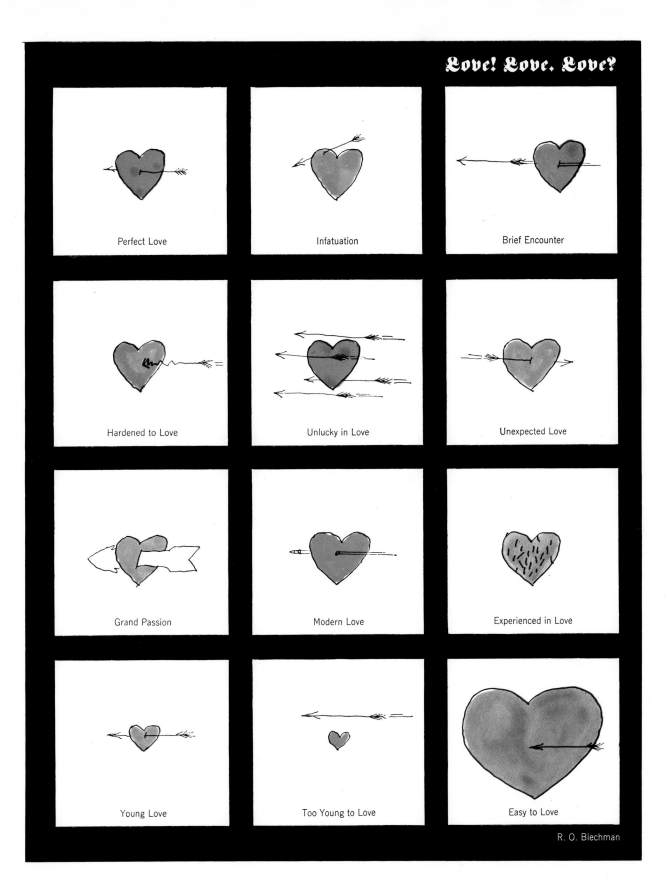

Perfect Love

Infatuation

Brief Encounter

Hardened to Love

Unlucky in Love

Unexpected Love

Grand Passion

Modern Love

Experienced in Love

Young Love

Too Young to Love

Easy to Love

R. O. Blechman

THEATRE ARTS

Theatre USA by Nan Martin

Michel de Ghelderode by Jack Richardson

Complete Play: Pantagleize

**My Rabbi
Doesn't Make
House Calls**

A Guide to Games
Jews Play

Albert Vorspan

Have him read the Song of Songs,
take a glass of wine,
and call me tomorrow

ISRAEL HOROVITZ

First
Season

PREVIEWS

Magazine cover,
Prisme International,
1968 [left].

Magazine cover,
Theatre Arts, 1962.

Book jacket,
*My Rabbi Doesn't Make
House Calls*, 1969.

Unpublished
sketch for book jacket,
1969.

Section opener,
"Previews,"
Show magazine, 1961.

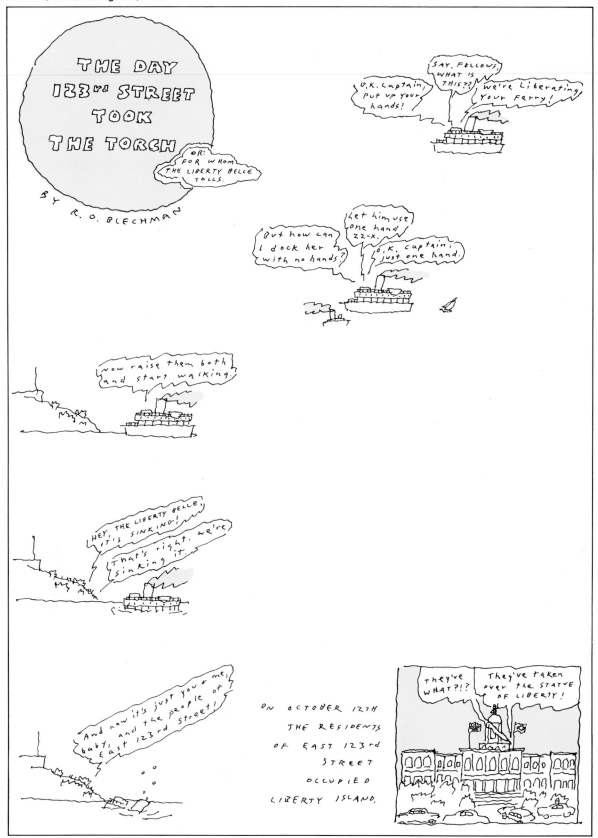

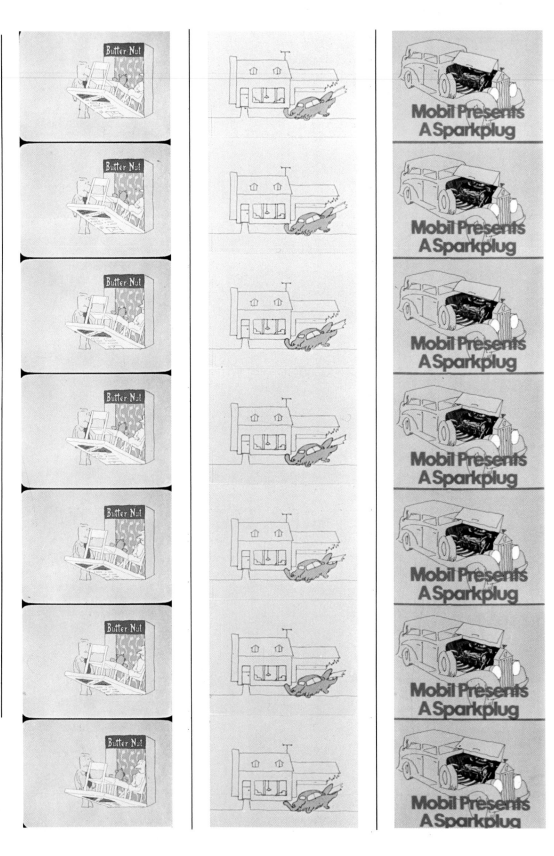

Animated television
commercials
[from left to right]:
Pan Am, 1969
Butter-Nut coffee, 1968
Volvo, 1968; Mobil, 1971
Alka-Seltzer, 1967
CBS (Season's Greetings), 1968
Mobil, 1971

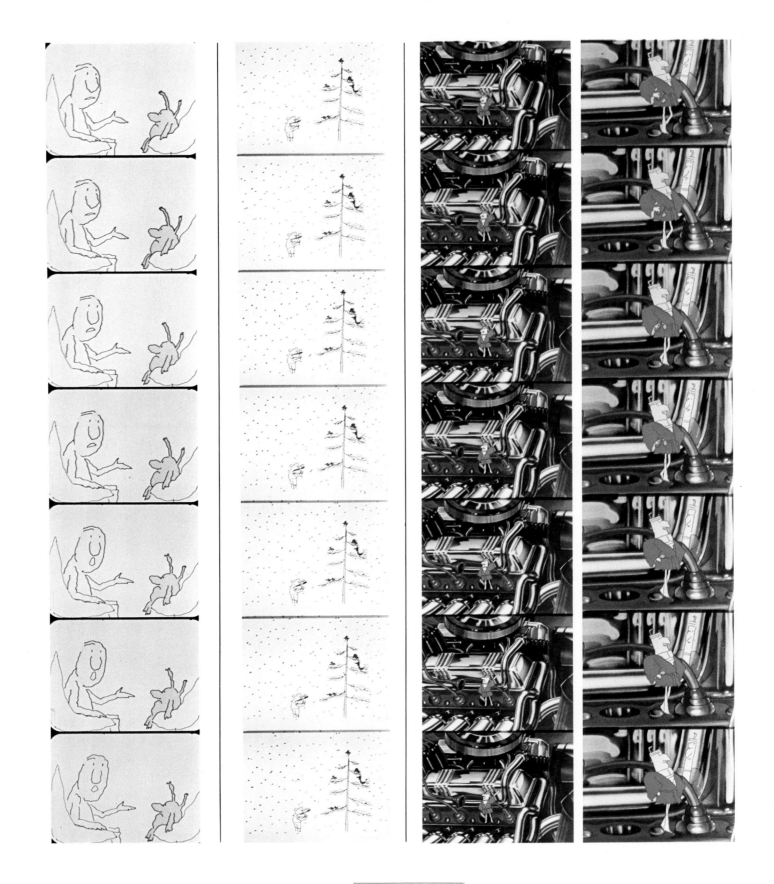

Unpublished sketch for car card, National Council on Alcoholism, 1964.

Newspaper ad for *TV Guide*, "How Big Is Best?," 1969.

My redesign of the dollar bill, *Avant Garde* magazine, 1968.

Illustration, *Show* magazine, 1963 [right].

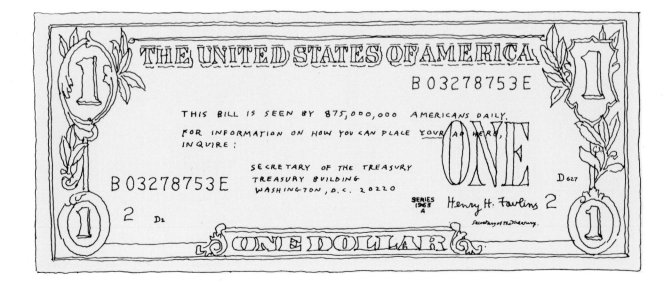

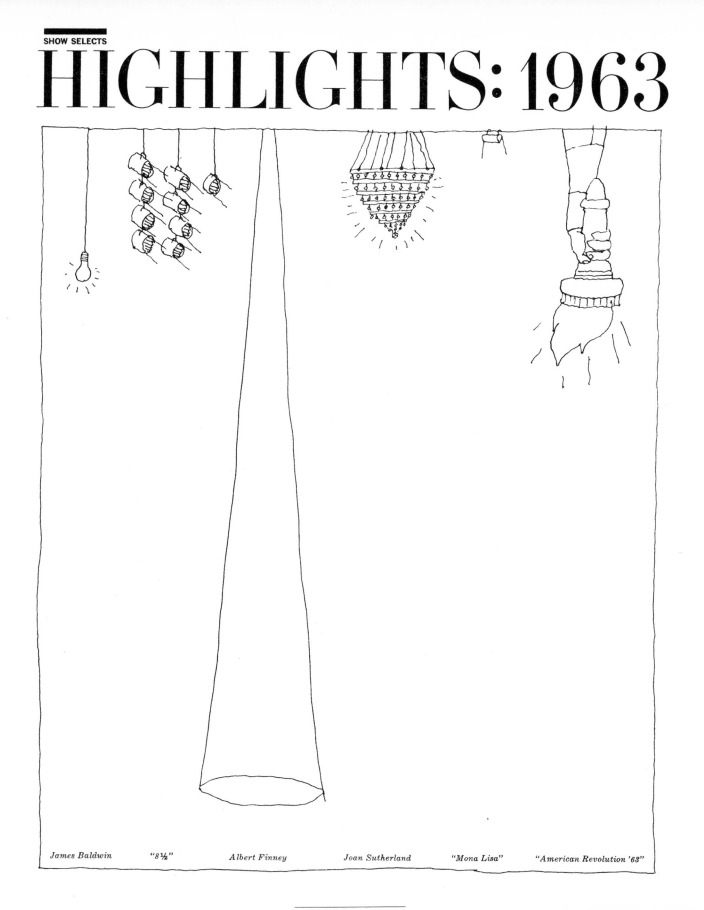

James Baldwin   "8½"   Albert Finney   Joan Sutherland   "Mona Lisa"   "American Revolution '63"

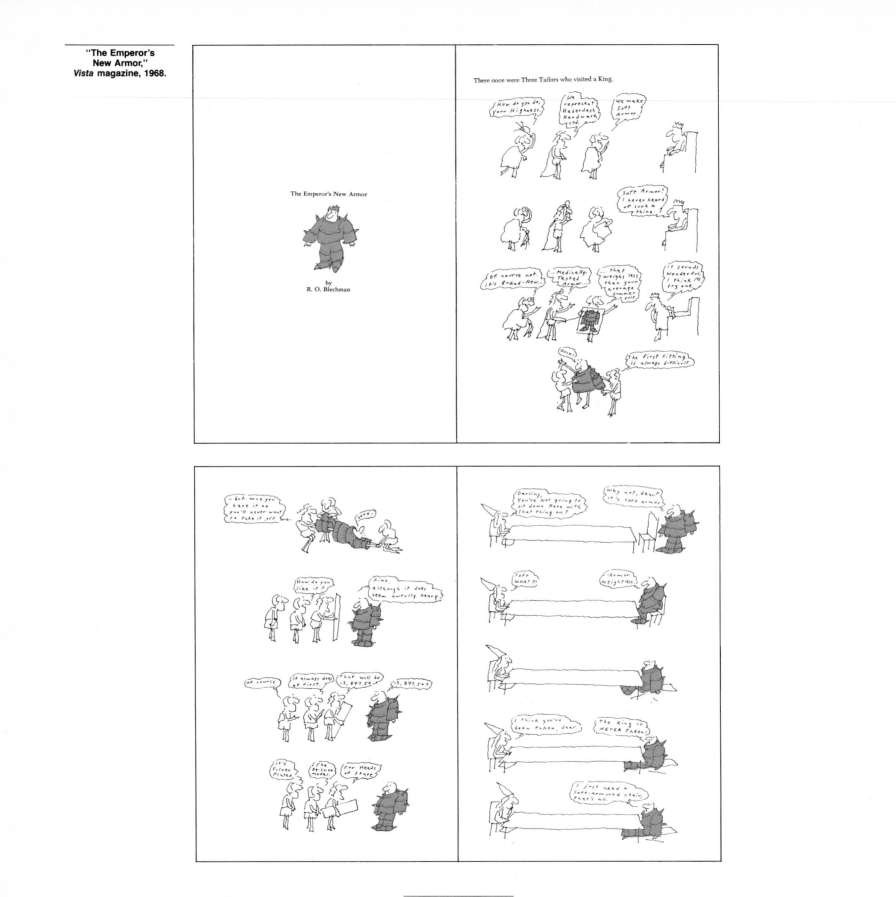

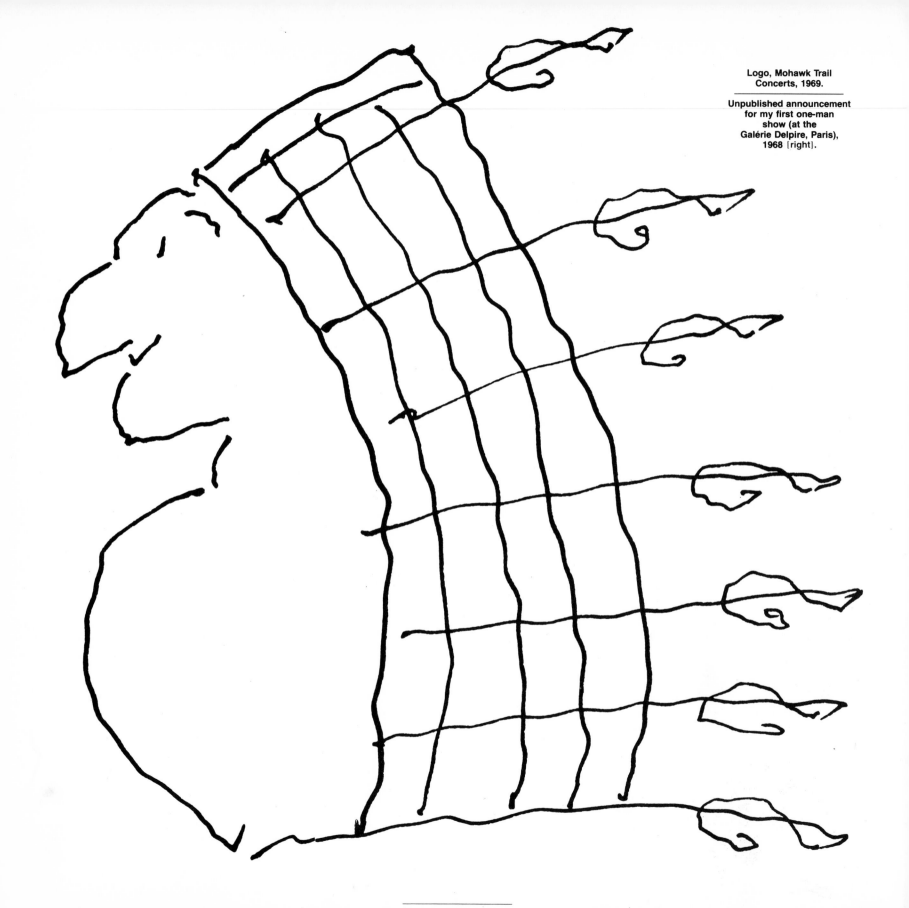

Logo, Mohawk Trail
Concerts, 1969.

Unpublished announcement
for my first one-man
show (at the
Galérie Delpire, Paris),
1968 [right].

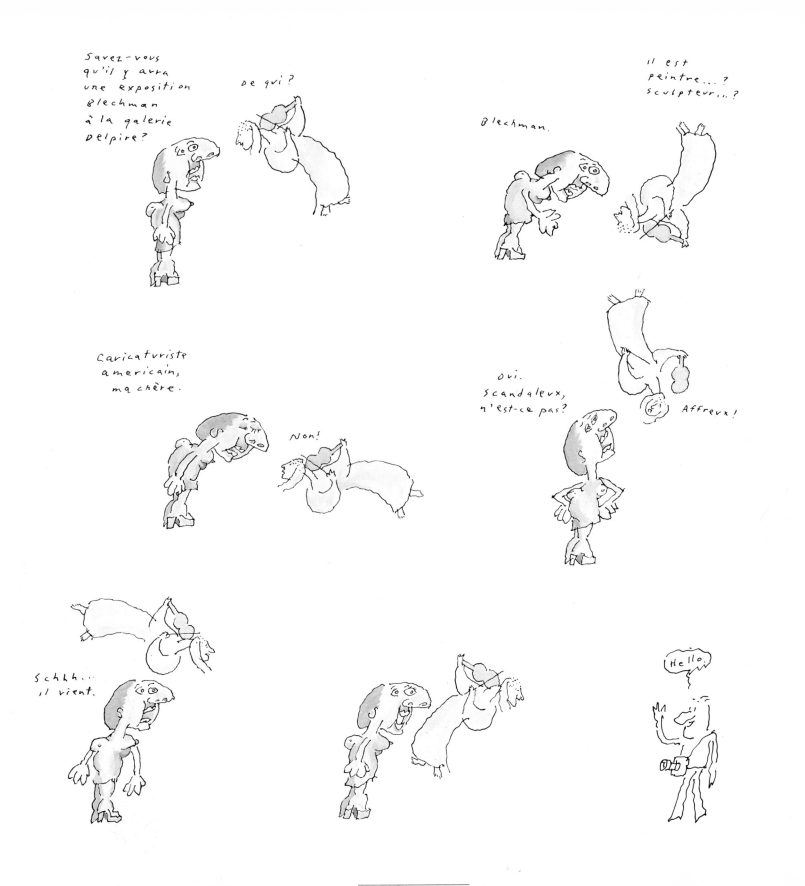

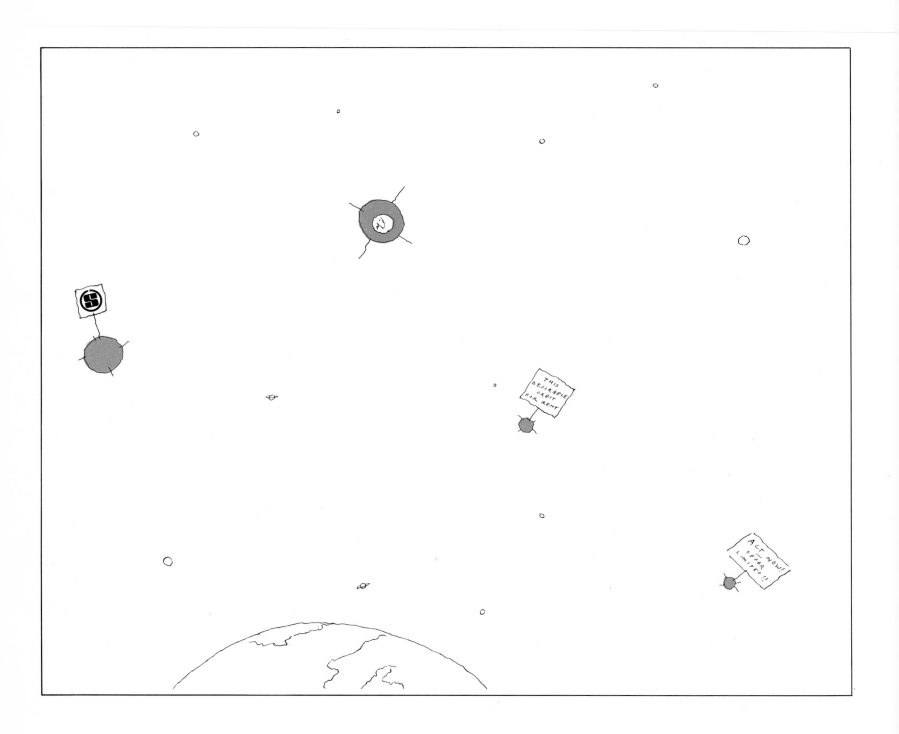

**Booklet cover, Space
Applications Corporation, 1969.**

**Advertisements,
Kaufman Carpet Company, 1964** [right].

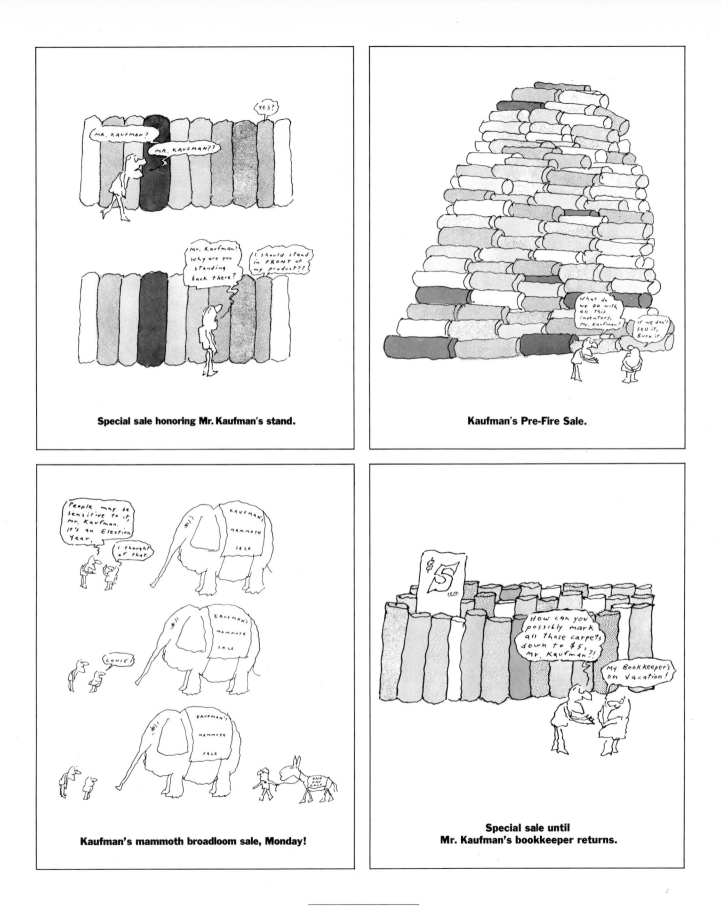

Special sale honoring Mr. Kaufman's stand.

Kaufman's Pre-Fire Sale.

Kaufman's mammoth broadloom sale, Monday!

**Special sale until
Mr. Kaufman's bookkeeper returns.**

BAZAAR
AWARDS

Host of the Year:
Mayor Daley

Telephone Number of the Year:
911

The Luxury of the Year:
Fresh air

Put-On of the Year:
Hair

Fashion of the Year:
Men

Bore of the Year:
The Pill

Cliché of the Year:
"Your own Thing"

Party of the Year:
Miami

Merger of the Year:
Westinghouse and Universal Pictures

Love of the Year:
Czechoslovakia

Drawings by R. O. Blechman

Scientist,

MEET THE PRESS

A Practical Guide To Press Relations
For Scientists And Technical Personnel

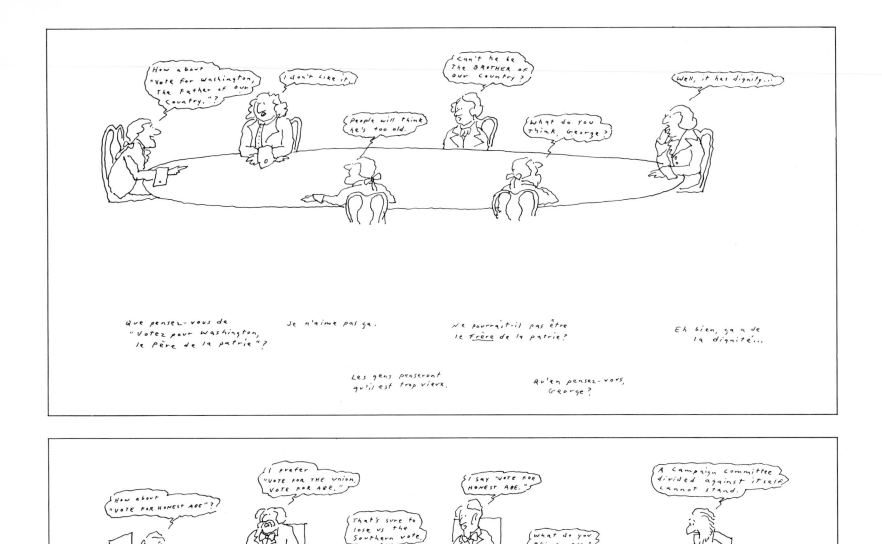

Que pensez-vous de "Votez pour Washington, le Père de la patrie"?

Je n'aime pas ça.

Ne pourrait-il pas être le Frère de la patrie?

Eh bien, ça a de la dignité...

Les gens penseront qu'il est trop vieux.

Qu'en pensez-vous, George?

Que pensez-vous de "Votez pour l'honnête Abe"?

J'aimerais mieux "Votez pour l'Union, votez pour Abe".

Je suis pour "Votez pour l'honnête Abe".

Un comité de campagne politique où règne la division ne saurait tenir.

Ça nous ferait sûrement perdre le suffrage du Sud.

Qu'en pensez-vous, Abe?

**Murals for the
American Pavilion, Expo 67.
(The Eisenhower mural
was removed
shortly before the opening.)**

**Uncle Sam mural for Expo 67.
(The cut-out lapel
button reveals alternating
elephant and donkey.)**

The Seventies

It began as an impish thought. What if I took The Greatest Story Ever Told and retold it in pictures? For years I had turned the Story over and over in my mind, attracted to the exquisite irony of the good citizens of Bethlehem rejecting the beggarly Joseph and Mary, only to see the light, quite literally, with the appearance of the Star of Bethlehem, ultimately making of them the central figures of a new religion. I played with the idea, finally drawing it up in a 24-page booklet of pencil drawings, which I brought to Milan when I went on other business.

I showed the booklet to Giovanni Gandini, an Italian publisher of marvelous originality and wit (he was later to publish a splendid *Little Nemo* collection). "Ver-ry good," he said, basso profundo. "But," he pointed to the thin dummy containing only one episode of the Christmas story, "what else will you do?" "I'll take 'The Visit of the Magi,' " I improvised, " 'Herod's Dream,' 'The Massacre of the Innocents' " (now I was warming up to the idea), "maybe 'The Flight into Egypt.' " "Okay, okay, Bobba," he answered ("Bobba" was my Italian name, as "Bub" was my French one), "do it."

Tutto Esaurito ("No Vacancies"), as it was to be called, drew its spirit and setting from the disordered decade we had just passed through. The hedonism, implied in the Fifties notion of The Good Life, had finally burst through in the Sixties. From every spray can and marker, kids let freedom ring. Adults honked automobile horns for Jesus or Sex, and bumper stickers demanded The Right to Live or to Pull the Plug, to Free the POW's or to Love America or Leave It! Americans did not so much argue their passions as flash them in belligerent split seconds (which allowed no rebuttal, but who cared what other people thought?).

In *Tutto Esaurito* I freely mixed architectural styles drawn from the visual Babel of my Central Park West neighborhood, outrageous costumes, and languages ranging from Italian and Russian to Japanese and French. Dissonance and discord were my motifs. But while the scene was pure Sixties, the underlying sadness was a Thirties loss of moral center and social purpose.

I returned to films that same year, 1971, again to work with ma-terial from the Bible. By now I had moved from my *La Bohème* studio to a more functional setup that I shared with two filmmakers. A producer from "The Great American Dream Machine" commissioned me to do a segment for the program. I felt compelled to deal with that most agonizing of issues, the Vietnam War. I handled the subject metaphorically by retelling the story of Abraham who was called upon to sacrifice his only son, Isaac. I had always been drawn to the father-son theme, and the idea of a father blindly killing his own (and sometimes only) son found its way into many of my stories. Probably my feeling for this material was heightened by the birth of my son (although I was younger than the 100-year-old Abraham).

"Abraham and Isaac" was one of the first films I produced. My inexperience showed not only in the film's technical errors, but also in the less forgivable creative errors I made. The film was to be a glorious failure. The marvelously lyric music, written by Arnold Black and performed by Pete Seeger, was matched neither by the stiff animation nor by the clumsy visuals.

I learned a great deal from "Abraham and Isaac" and applied these lessons to a far more technically accomplished film two years later. "Exercise," commissioned by the Children's Television Workshop, received its title not only because it dealt with physical exercise, but also because I considered it too unambitious to be more than a mere exercise. It marked my first collaboration with a master animator, Ed Smith. Whatever virtues the film possessed were largely due to his fluid and expressive handling of my characters as well as to Arnold Black's music. These two artists have been, ever since, close and trusted collaborators. And to Arnold Black (who maintains that he was a Blechman before Ellis Island transformed his family name) I was to dedicate a drawing: "To my ears, from your eyes."

I worked increasingly on commercials, and soon decided to move to a larger studio. Fate, in the form of a real estate crisis in New York, offered me a wonderful choice of spaces. I moved into the studio workshop of Bertram Goodhue, an early-twentieth-century architect who had specialized in church architecture. His studio might have served as a portfolio of his work. It had a triplex leaded-glass win-

dow, an arched ceiling elaborately decorated with putti and grape-vines, stained glass, and a walk-in fireplace stenciled with hortatory mottoes in Greek, Latin, and German. I moved into this place—or rather, a corner of it—feeling not unlike Cantalbert moving into a monastery. My sense of anomie was heightened by my neighbors, most of whom were Chassidic Jews working in the diamond industry.

Situated in my Kane-like aerie, later described by a colleague as a cold-water castle, I concentrated on the extravagant goal of making longer films. I was not to neglect more modest projects, however. In 1974, I did my first *New Yorker* cover, mostly for the sheer challenge of working again in watercolor. Later, I illustrated an edition of *Candide* for Olivetti with a series of wash drawings. The illustrations for *Candide*, as it turned out, were on the sweet and conventional side, as I wanted them to serve as models for a possible animated feature (which I could later pepper and salt more to Voltaire's recipe). Although my hands were on watercolor brushes and pens, my eyes were still wildly scanning the far horizons of film.

In 1976, Lawrence K. Grossman, owner of an advertising agency bearing his name, asked me to animate a fund-raising spot for the Public Broadcasting System. "Dreams That Money Can Buy" was its tag line. A dream that money could not buy was to be his that year: Grossman was chosen as president of the Public Broadcasting System. Sometime later we sat down to discuss a dream of my own: It was to produce a Christmas program using the work of artists I admired, each of whom would design a self-contained segment.

Within a month it had taken definite shape. I conceived of the program as a one-hour animated special consisting of seven widely varied segments unified by their Christmas subject matter. The artists included Maurice Sendak, whose story served as overture; Seymour Chwast, who visualized a section of Virginia Woolf's *Orlando*; James McMullan, whose watercolors pictured a short-lived truce during the First World War; Chas. B. Slackman, whose crosshatched drawings evoked a moment from young Teddy Roosevelt's Christmas; and me, adapting *Tutto*

Esaurito.

In the tripartite setup of Public Broadcasting, where local member stations, PBS (the administrative arm of the system), and CPB (the funding arm) carried federalism to an ultimate absurdity, the funding process was to be slow and baffling. But grant by grant, the funding was made. Two years after the initial proposal was written, the final payment came through and I was able to finish a production that I had rashly undertaken with money of my own.

"Simple Gifts," as it was to be called for lack of a better title, was to have a photo-finish ending. I had invested most of my time and energy in segments other than my own, and two months before the program was to be aired I realized that Ed Smith was still moving Joseph and Mary through the higher-class inns of Bethlehem. Clearly, by the time he got them to the manger, Christmas would have come and gone. I frantically hired other animators: one animated Herod's dream, another the marching elephants, another the birds of Egypt, and still another a flock of sheep. In all, there were seven animators scrambling about the studio trying to tie up the ribbons for our Christmas gift to America. A few days before the deadline, the film was completed. Joseph was to reach Egypt with his cane missing every fourth step (an animator's error: in the last-minute rush to complete the film, Joseph's staff was omitted every sixteenth drawing).

It irked me terribly at the time, that missing staff, but it was too late—I had neither the time nor the budget to redo it. But it did not finally matter, this missing staff, so glaringly evident to me, but which nobody else seemed to notice (except for a few animators, one of whom saw it as a highlight on the staff—"a brilliant touch!" he said). What mattered really was that Joseph reached Egypt, and that I had reached the air date with my vision of the program mostly intact.

"Simple Gifts" was to be a way station. The day after the program was aired, the large-screen color TV I had rented for the occasion was returned. I set on the road again—no, it was not a road. There was no road because nobody had preceded me on the journey I was to take—I simply set out, that is all, with a staff that I hoped would not fail me every fourth step of the way.

L-1
(starting position)

L-2
(final position)

**Illustration for
poster announcing my lecture,
"From Print to Film,"
Boston Art Directors Club,
1978.**

Unpublished comic strip, 1972. (The first panel is missing.)

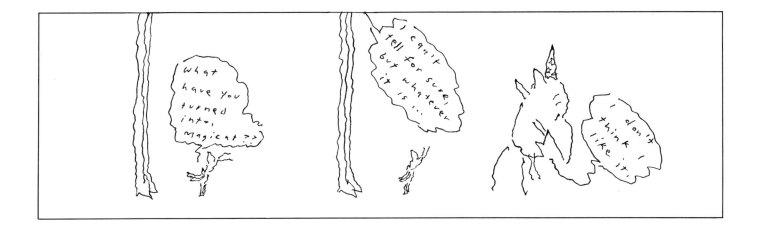

Unpublished sketch on the judiciary, 1978.

**Cover illustration on
the FBI infiltration of the Black Panthers,
New York Times Book Review, 1973.**

Illustration for article "The Greening of America," *Mother Jones* magazine, 1976.

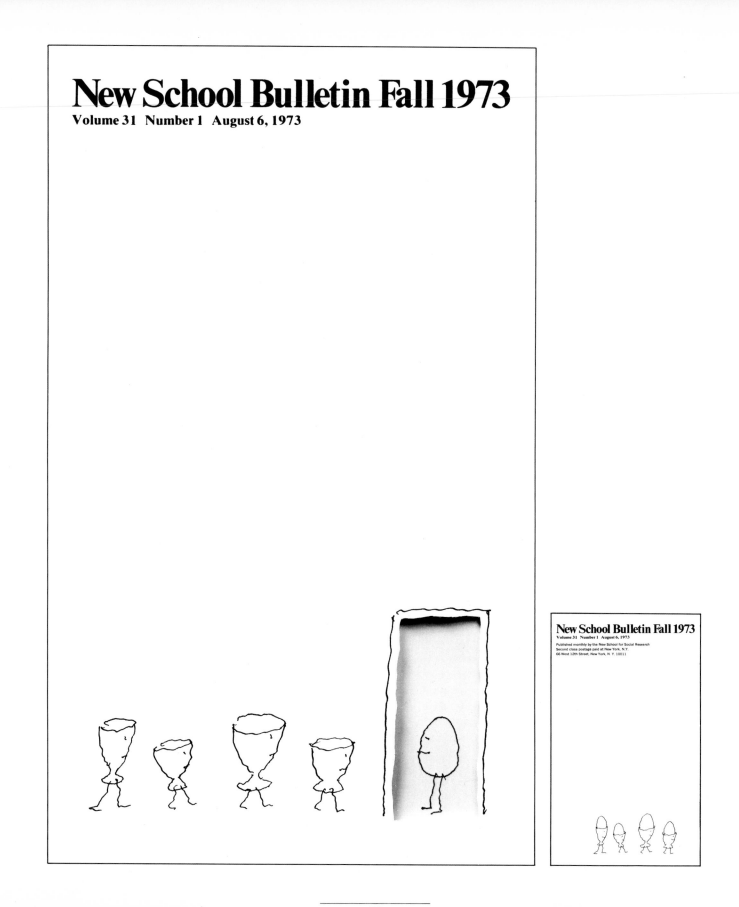

New School Bulletin Fall 1973

Volume 31 Number 1 August 6, 1973

New School Bulletin Fall 1973

Volume 31 Number 1 August 6, 1973

Published monthly by the New School for Social Research
Second class postage paid at New York, N.Y.
66 West 12th Street, New York, N.Y. 10011

Die-cut cover
and title page for the
New School Bulletin,
1973 [left].

Illustration announcing
the show
"Communicating with Children,"
American Institute
of Graphic Arts, 1979.

Subway cards,
Irving Trust Company, 1970 [left].

Illustration
for newspaper ad,
Georgia Bank, 1973.

**Illustration for
a book review about loyalist
refugees during
the Revolutionary War,**
***New York Times
Book Review,*** **1973.**

Illustrations,
Horticulture **magazine,**
1977 [top right].

**Illustration for article
"Washington and Slavery,"**
New York Times, **1973
[bottom right].**

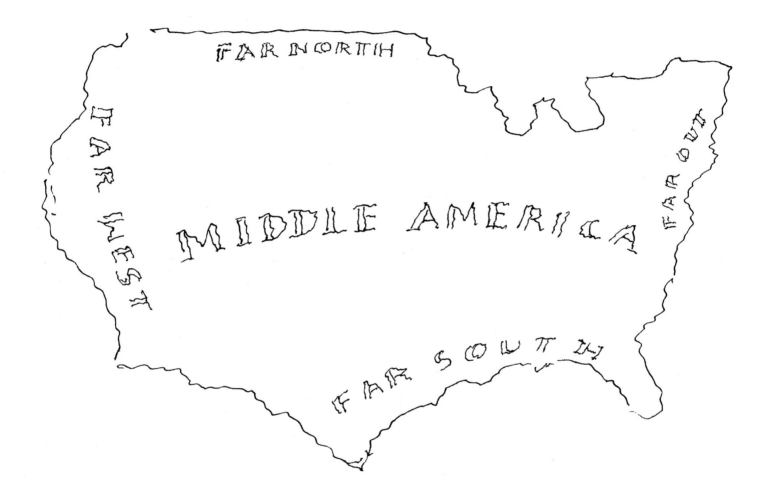

FAR NORTH

FAR WEST

FAR OUT

MIDDLE AMERICA

FAR SOUTH

Unpublished drawing, 1977.

Storyboard for
proposed feature film
The Golden Ass, 1979 [**right**].

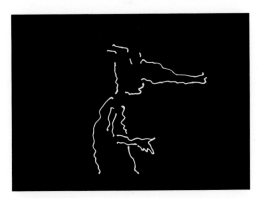  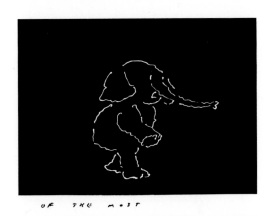

(VOICE : O.S.)
(OVER BLACK)   IF YOU ARE NOT PUT OFF   BY A STORY IN WHICH   HUMANS

CHANGE   INTO CREATURES   OF THE MOST

EXTRA ORDINARY   — AND ORDINARY —   KIND, ...

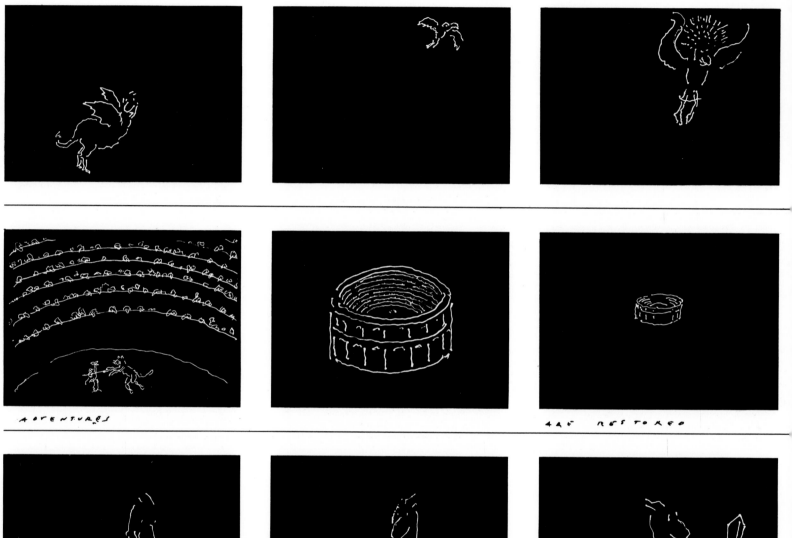

ADVENTURES

ARE RESTORED

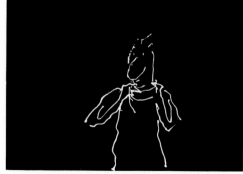

YOU WILL BE ENTERTAINED
BY MY STORY.

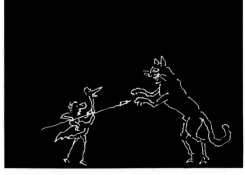

~ AND AFTER MANY

TO THEIR ORIGINAL SHAPES, ...

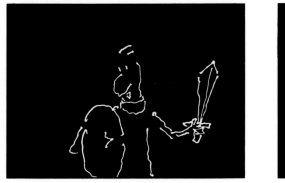

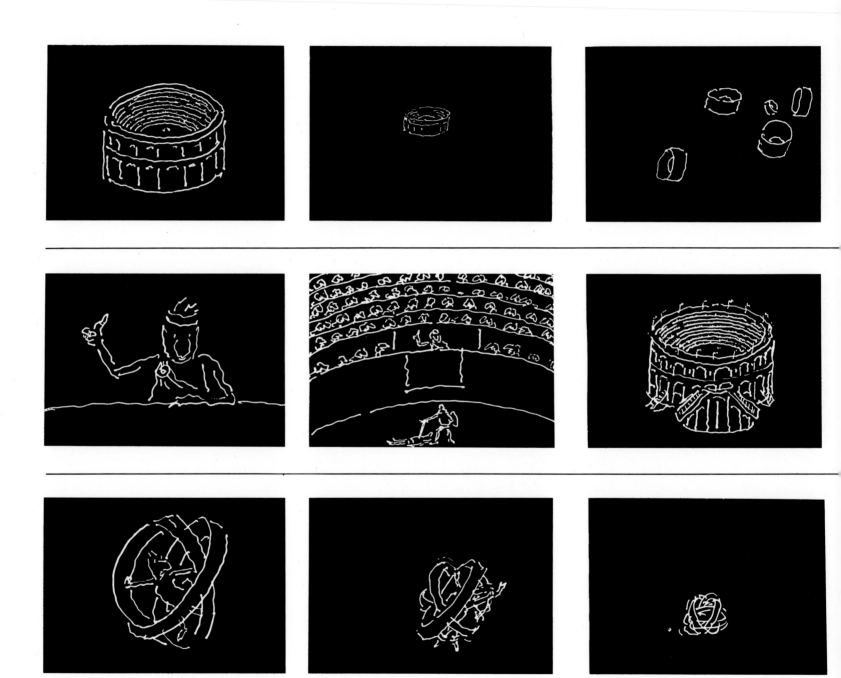

I CALL THIS STORY... MY "TRANSFORMATIONS"

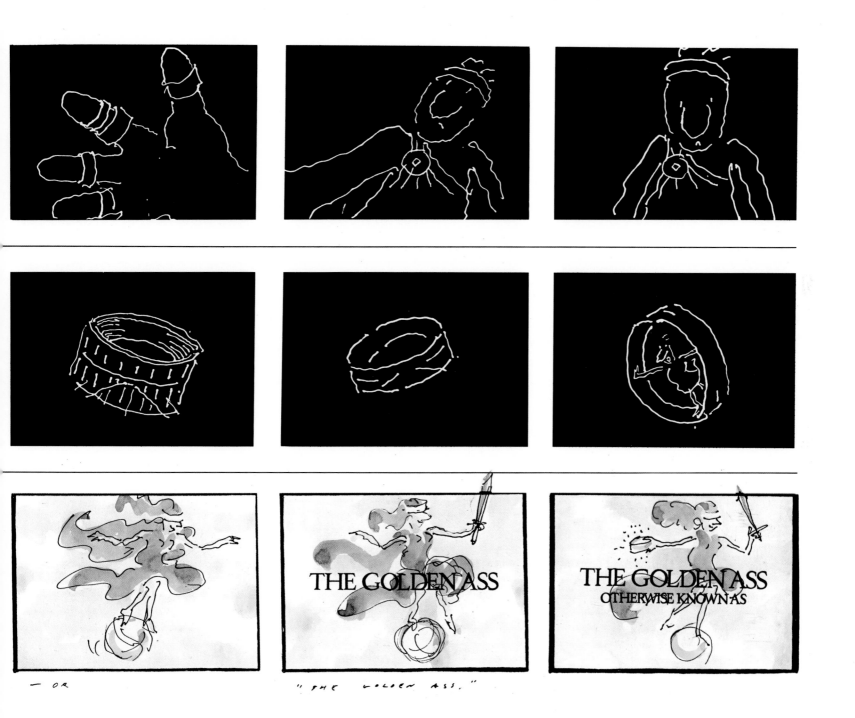

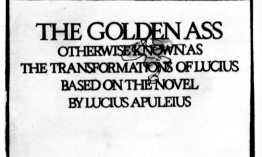

THE GOLDEN ASS
OTHERWISE KNOWN AS
THE TRANSFORMATIONS OF LUCIUS

THE GOLDEN ASS
OTHERWISE KNOWN AS
THE TRANSFORMATIONS OF LUCIUS
BASED ON THE NOVEL

THE GOLDEN ASS
OTHERWISE KNOWN AS
THE TRANSFORMATIONS OF LUCIUS
BASED ON THE NOVEL
BY LUCIUS APULEIUS

(TITLES ROLL)

... WHERE MY MOTHER'S FAMILY

OTHERWISE KNOWN AS
THE TRANSFORMATIONS OF LUCIUS
BASED ON THE NOVEL
BY LUCIUS APULEIUS,
2ND CENTURY A.D.

BUSINESS ONCE TOOK ME ...   TO THESSALY ...

IT WAS IN THIS DESOLATE PLACE

THAT I CAME ACROSS TWO MEN,

DEEP IN CONVERSATION

1.
THE STORY OF ARISTOMENES

(1ST MAN:) "IMPOSSIBLE! I CAN'T BEAR YOUR ABSURD AND MONSTROUS LIES!"

SONY TAPE.
FULL COLOR
SOUND.

Four covers,
New Yorker magazine [**left**].

Poster and cover,
New Yorker magazine, 1979.

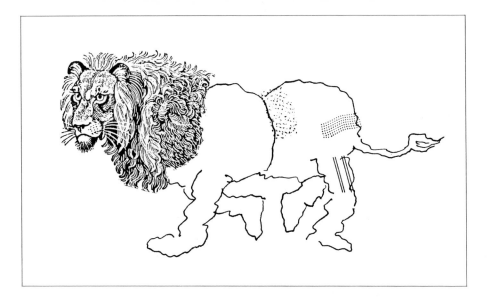

The True History of the Potato by R. O. Blechman

Sir Pettibone Potato was a celebrated Botanist of 17th century England.

Among his discoveries were the Bananberry & the Liquid-Core Apple.

But during the reign of Oliver Cromwell the national taste changed.

Eager to change with the times, Sir Pettibone labored many years...

... to produce a Flat, Tasteless, Odorless Vegetable

However, the national taste had changed again.

Sir Pettibone Potato died a broken-hearted man, his vegetable ignored...

...until many years later, when plainer tastes prevailed.

A Grateful Nation erected a simple Granite Potato to mark his grave.

Page from
The Potato Book,
William Morrow & Co., 1972
[far left].

Illustration for
''Hot Seasonings,''
New York Times, 1978.

Storyboards for unproduced public service television spots, "Bible Minutes," 1976.

1. The Creation of the World

(NARRATOR:) ON THE FIRST DAY

HE CREATED THE EARTH.

ON THE THIRD DAY

GOD CREATED THE SUN

THE FIFTH DAY GOD CREATED THE

ANIMALS.

(FINGER TURNS TOWARD VIEWER) AND ON THE SIXTH DAY GOD CREATE

(MAN:) HELLO?

GOD?

PULL BACK

ARE YOU RESTING, GOD?

GOD

CREATED THE

HEAVENS. ON THE SECOND DAY

AND THE MOON.

PULL IN

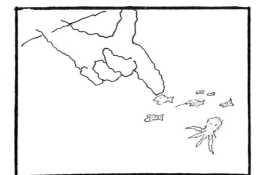

ON THE FOURTH DAY
HE CREATED THE FISH

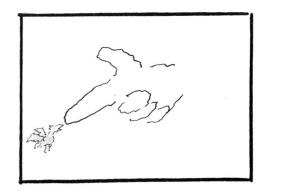

AND THE FOWL. ON

MAN.

(THE HAND OF GOD EXITS)

HELLO?

MAYBE HE'LL RETURN
ON THE EIGHTH DAY.

MAYBE NOT.

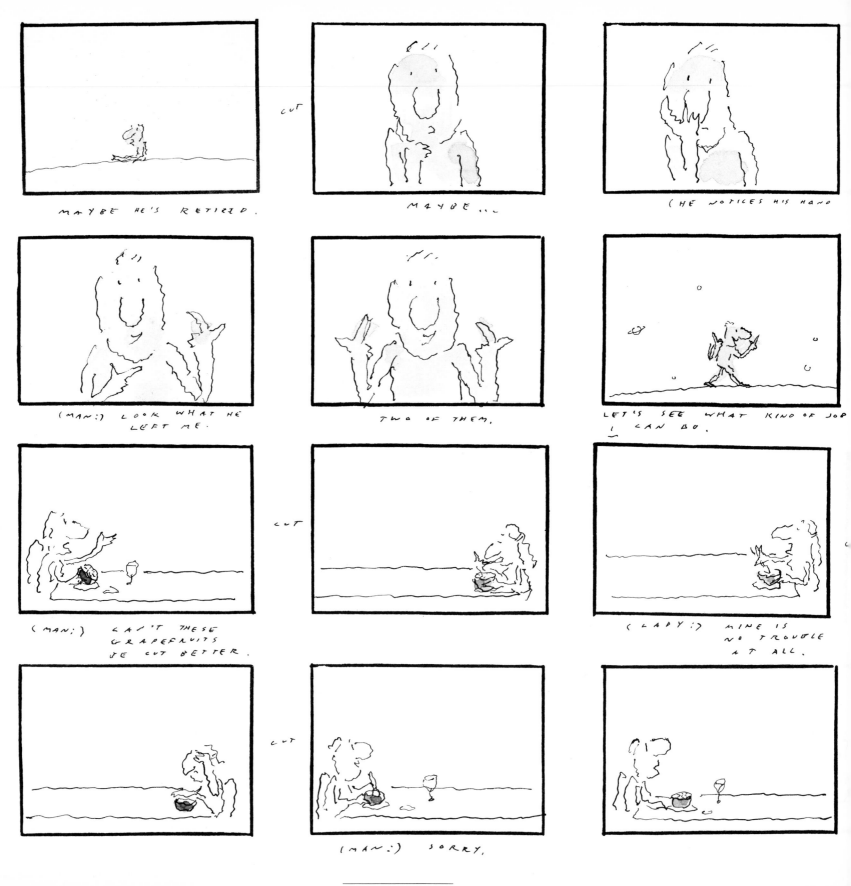

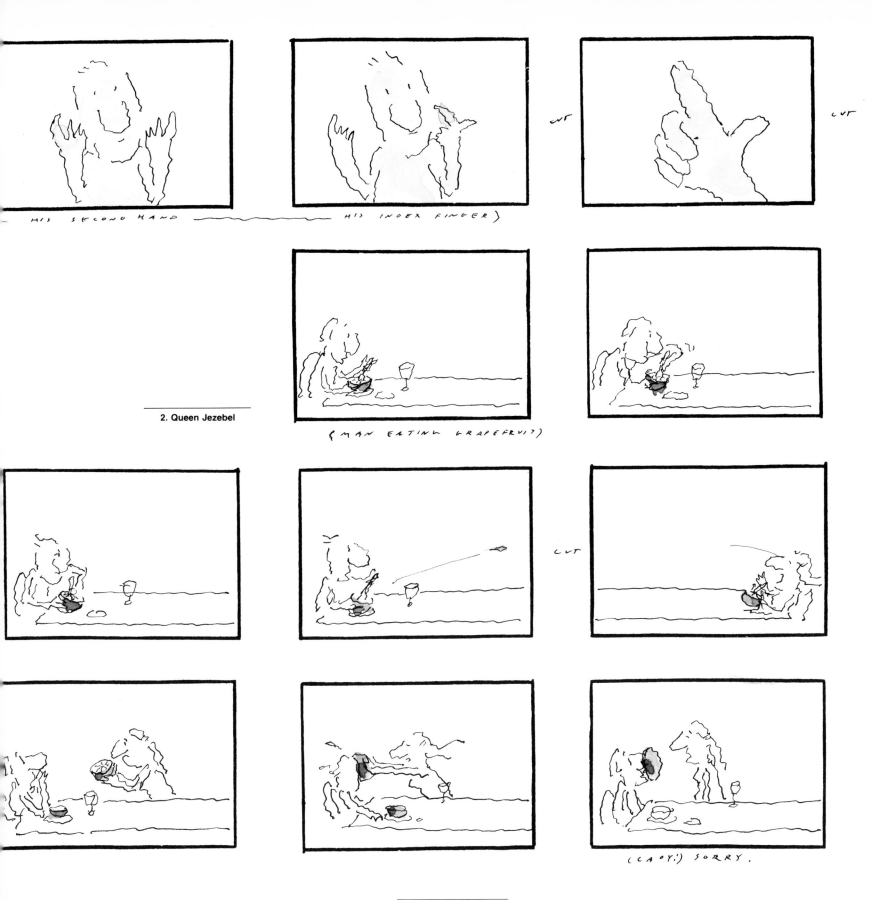

HIS SECOND HAND ——————————— HIS INDEX FINGER)

CUT   CUT

2. Queen Jezebel

(MAN EATING GRAPEFRUIT)

CUT

(CONT.) SORRY.

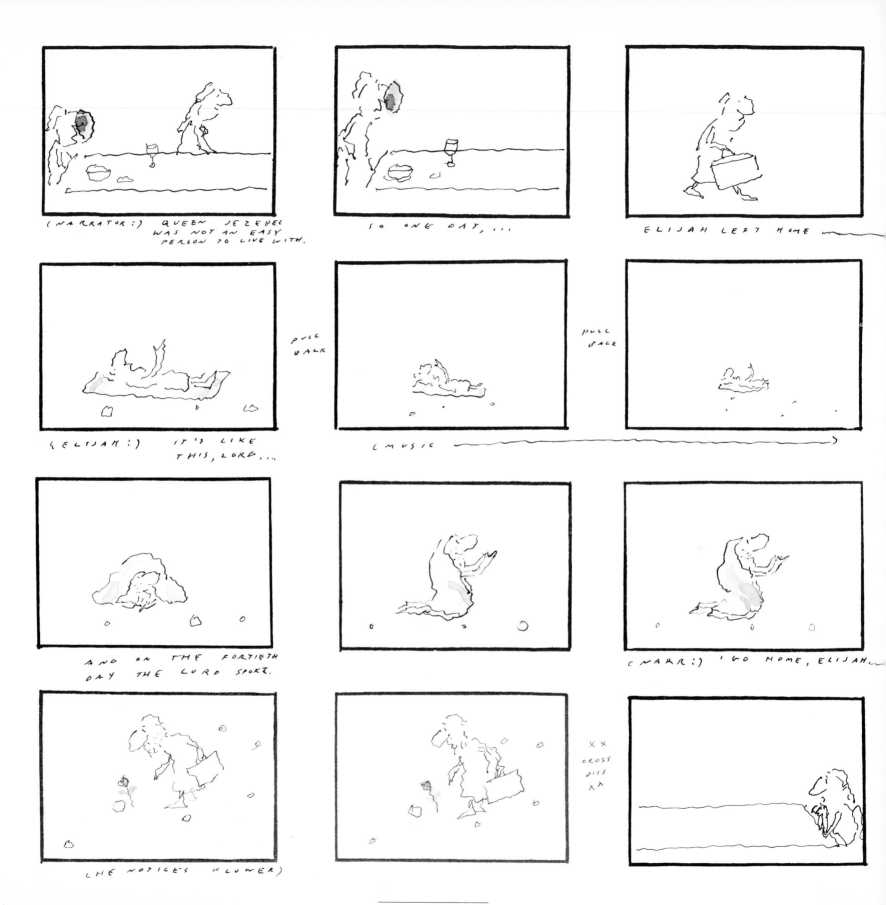

140

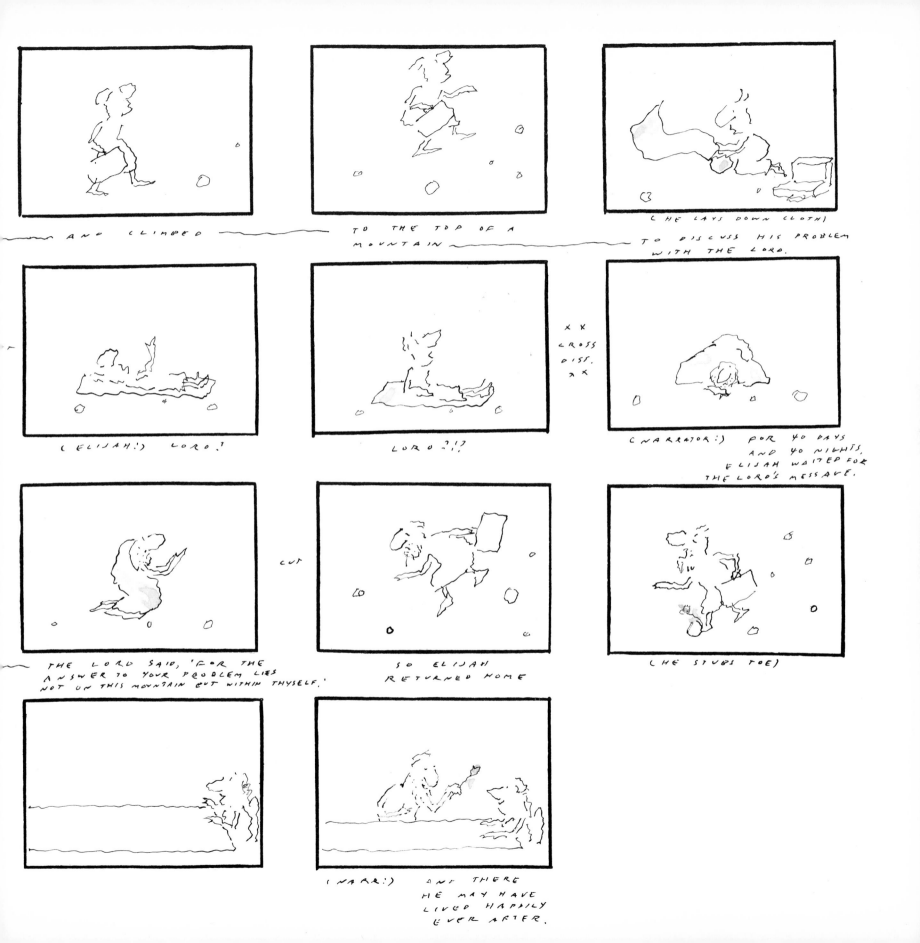

AND CLIMBED

TO THE TOP OF A
MOUNTAIN

(HE LAYS DOWN CLOTH)
TO DISCUSS HIS PROBLEM
WITH THE LORD.

(ELIJAH!) LORD!

LORD ?!?

X X
CROSS
DISS.
X X

(NARRATOR:) FOR 40 DAYS
AND 40 NIGHTS,
ELIJAH WAITED FOR
THE LORD'S MESSAGE.

THE LORD SAID, 'FOR THE
ANSWER TO YOUR PROBLEM LIES
NOT ON THIS MOUNTAIN BUT WITHIN THYSELF.'

CUT

SO ELIJAH
RETURNED HOME

(HE STUBS TOE)

(NARR:) AND THERE
HE MAY HAVE
LIVED HAPPILY
EVER AFTER.

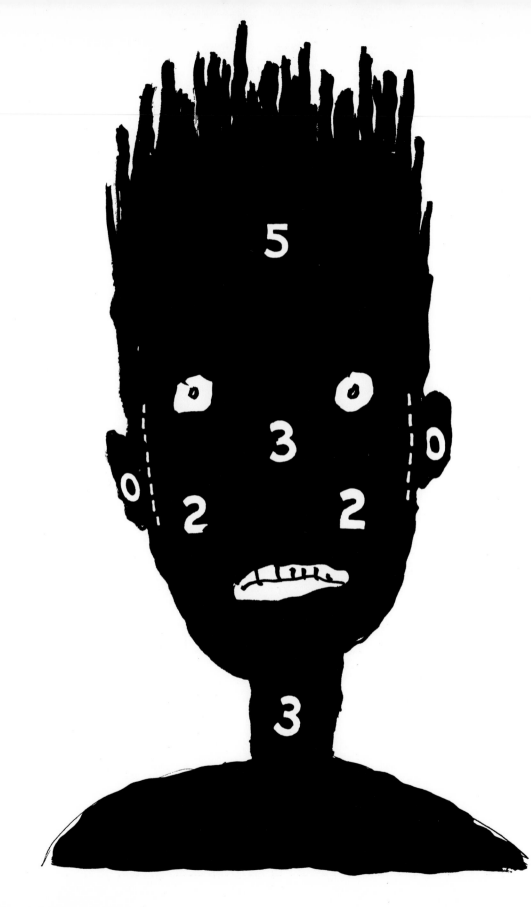

Illustration for article
"Yes, But Who—Who?—
Fires the Administrators?"
New York Times, 1976.

Illustration for article
"The Chair Recognizes Senator
Saul Bellow of Illinois,"
New York Times, 1977.

Unpublished sketch, 1977
[top right].

Illustration from
the book *Systemantics*,
Quadrangle Books, 1977
[bottom right].

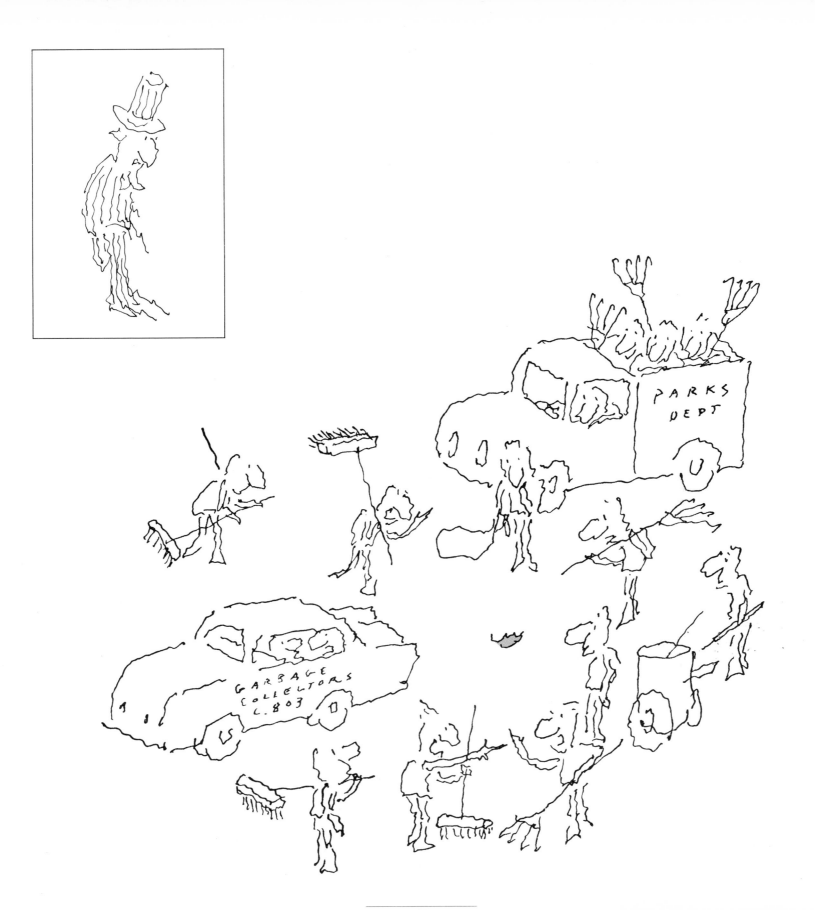

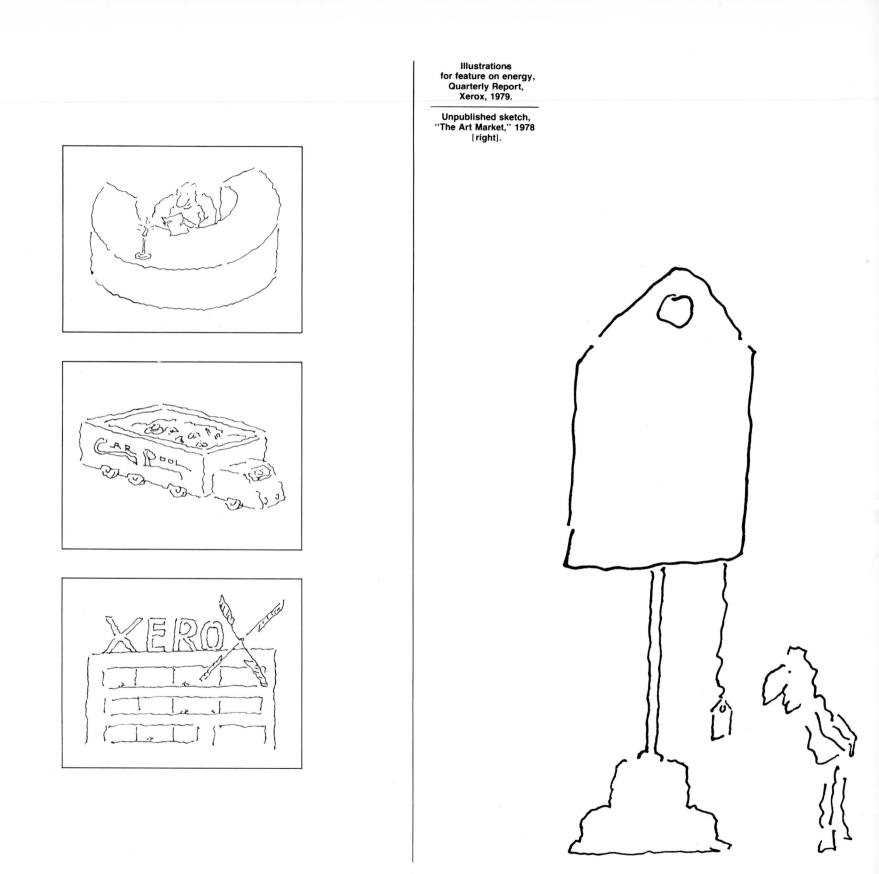

**Illustrations
for feature on energy,
Quarterly Report,
Xerox, 1979.**

**Unpublished sketch,
"The Art Market," 1978**
[right].

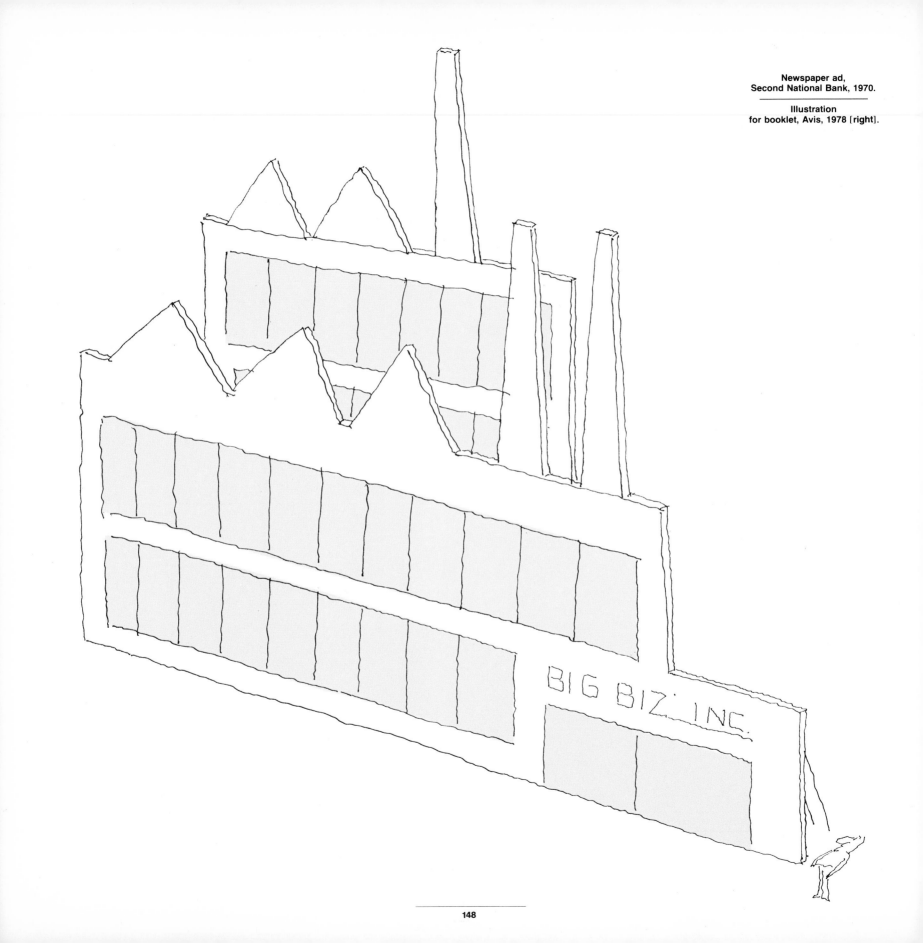

BIG BIZ INC.

Halloween feature, *New York Times Magazine*, 1976.

Illustrations for
"A Love/Hate Relationship with the City,"
New York **magazine, 1977.**

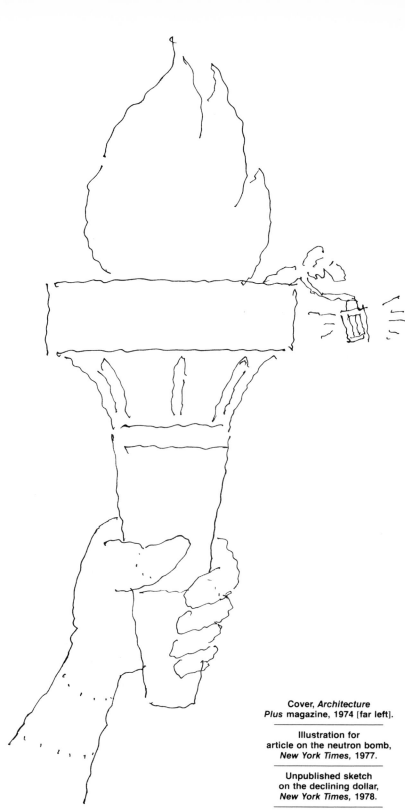

Cover, *Architecture Plus* magazine, 1974 [far left].

Illustration for article on the neutron bomb, *New York Times*, 1977.

Unpublished sketch on the declining dollar, *New York Times*, 1978.

Illustration for article lamenting the quality of the presidential nominees, *New York Times*, 1976.

Illustration for
article on tax cuts,
New York Times, 1976 [top left].

Illustration for
article "Freud's Disaster
with Cocaine,"
New York Times, 1972 [center left].

Illustration for
article on drop-outs,
New York Times, 1972 [bottom left].

Unpublished sketch
for article on
Governor Rockefeller's
anti-crime proposal,
New York Times, 1973.

The published illustration,
New York Times, 1973.

Illustrations
accompanying article
"Strategies for
High Market-Share Companies,"
Harvard Business Review, 1975 [left].

Illustration for
article on the British takeover
of Howard Johnson's,
New York Times, 1979.

Sketches for proposed
Op-Ed masthead at time of
Nixon's trip to Egypt,
New York Times, 1973.

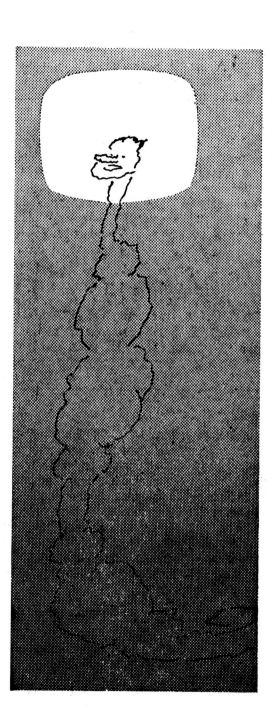

**Illustration for article
"Trial by Television,"
New York Times, 1977.**

**Unpublished sketch on
Nixon's resignation, 1973.**

**Illustration for article
"A Code of Loyalty,"
New York Times, 1973.**

Editorial cartoon
commenting on the accidental
napalm bombing of Vietnamese
civilians during the Nixon–McGovern
presidential race, *New York Times*, 1972.

Illustration for article
on Nixon's Vietnam peace plan
announced toward the close of his race for
re-election, *New York Times*, 1972.

Illustration for article on the medical fitness of presidents, *New York Times*, 1972.

Two illustrations
for article "I.Q. Tests on Trial,"
New York Times, 1978.

Illustration for
George Plimpton's
commencement address,
New York Times, 1977.

Illustration for article
on contemporary
poetry in America,
New York Times Magazine,
1980 [right].

9728344   9728345   9728346   9728347

Cover and illustrations,
Candide, or Optimism,
Olivetti, 1976.

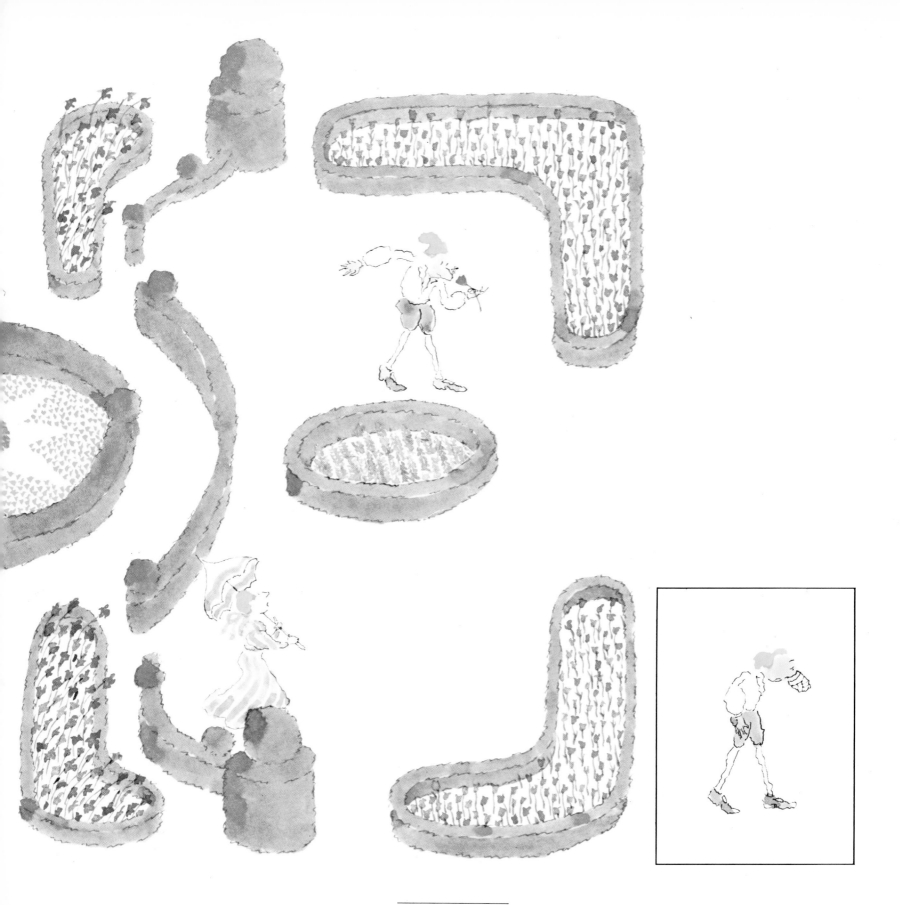

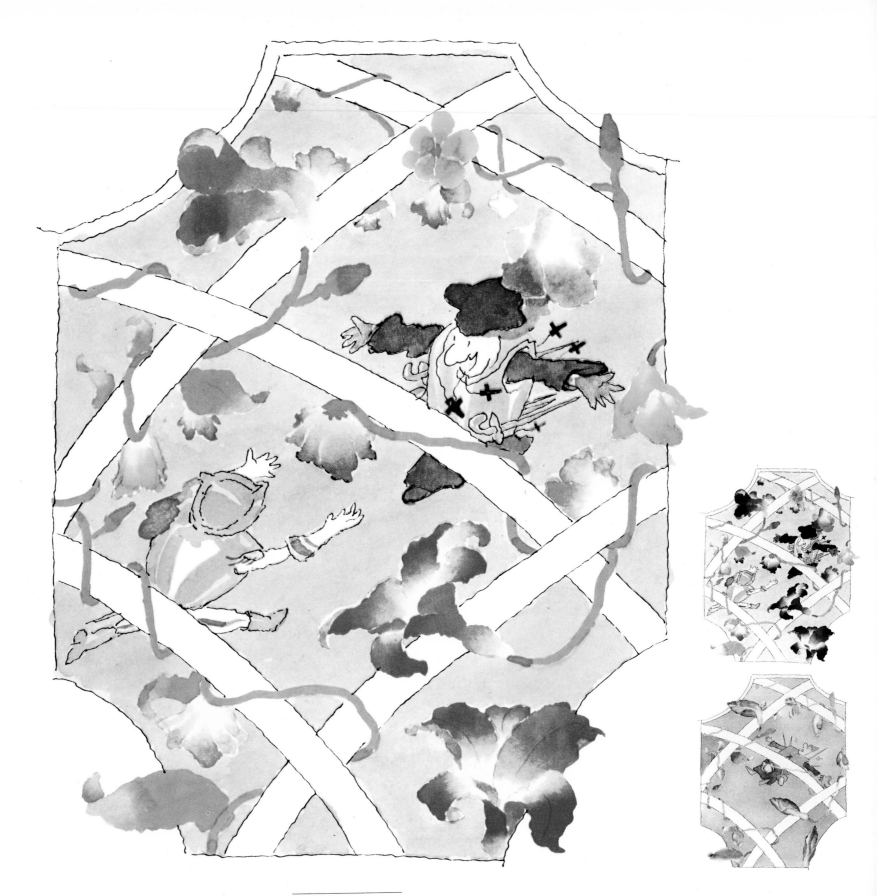

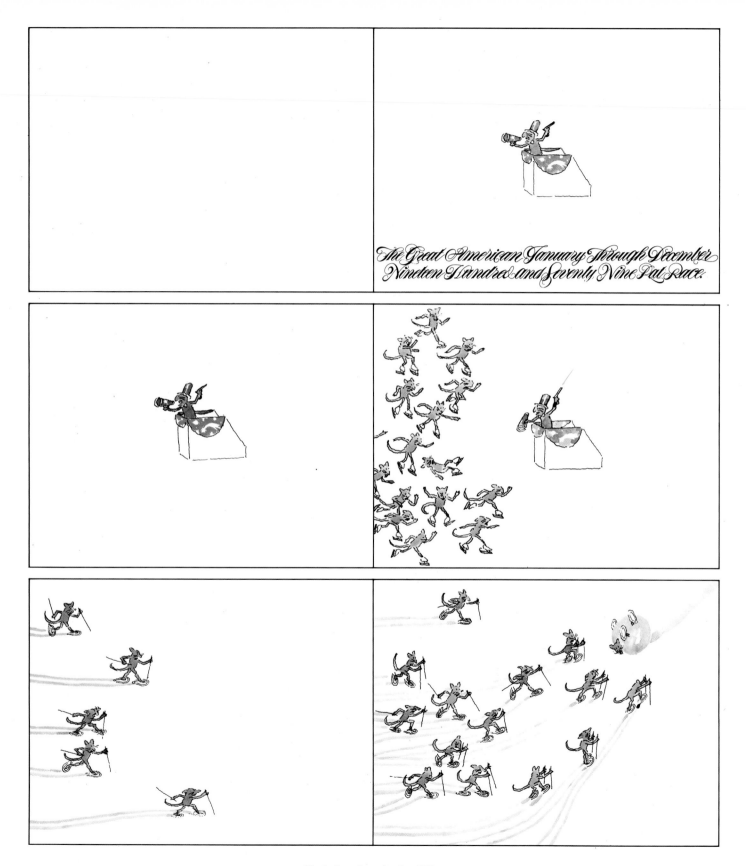

Illustrations for calendar, 1979.

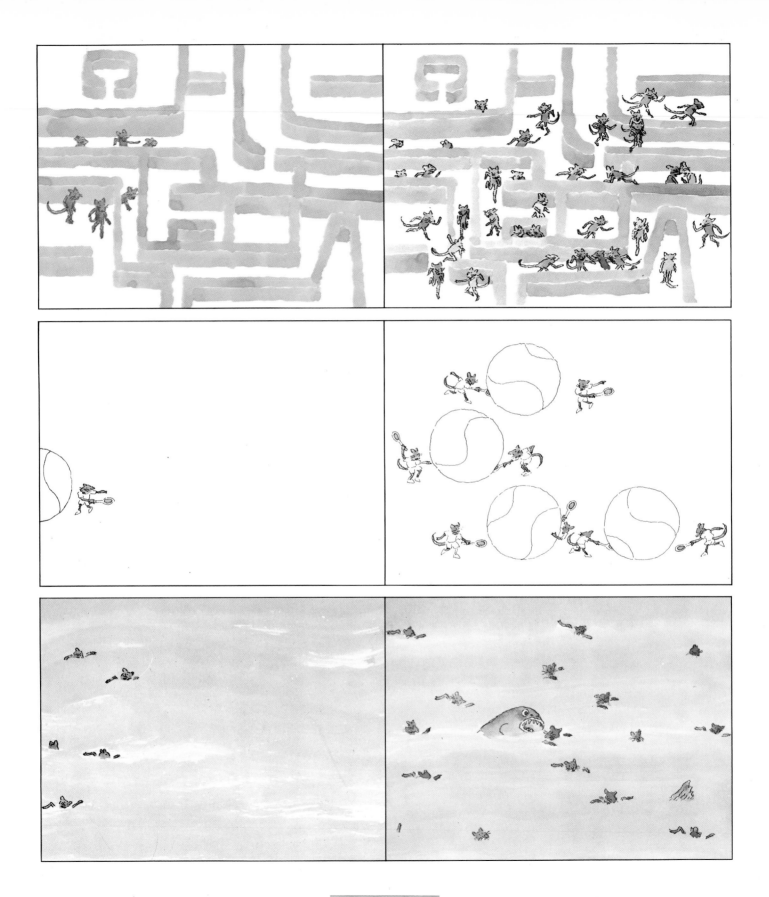

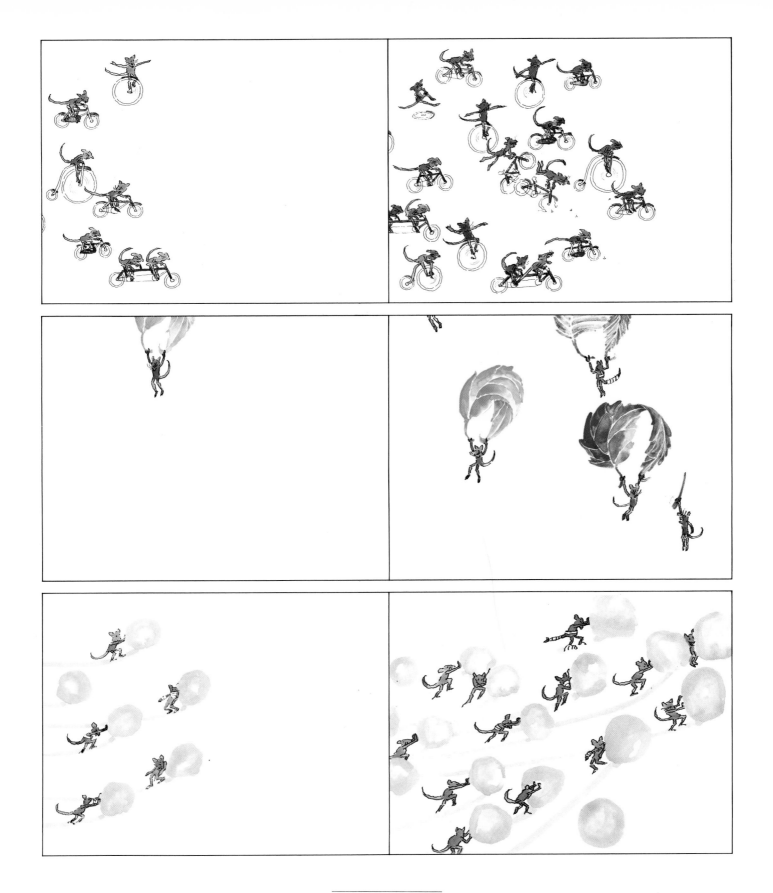

Illustration for an article on revisiting the Sixties, *Mother Jones* magazine, 1976.

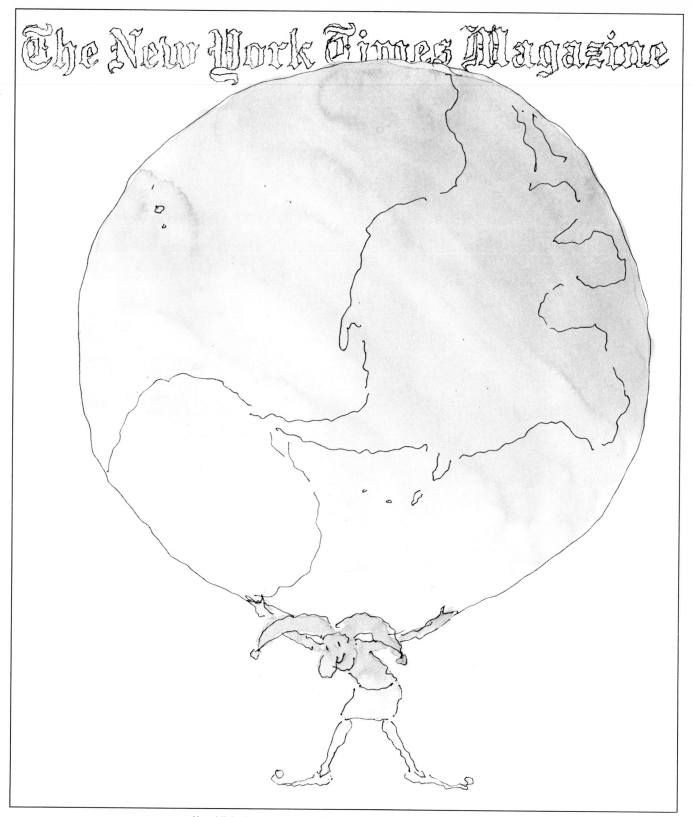

Unpublished cover sketch for feature article on the book *Systemantics*
(Or Why Things Don't Work as Well as They Ought to), New York Times Magazine, 1976.

Sketch for drawing published in *Politicks* magazine, 1978.

Illustration for article
"My Experiments with Truth—
Or My Search for the Perfect Guru,"
New York Times, 1971.

Illustration for article
"Kissed by a Gypsy
and an MG,"
New York Times, 1979 [top right].

Unpublished sketch
on judicial authority, 1978
[bottom right].

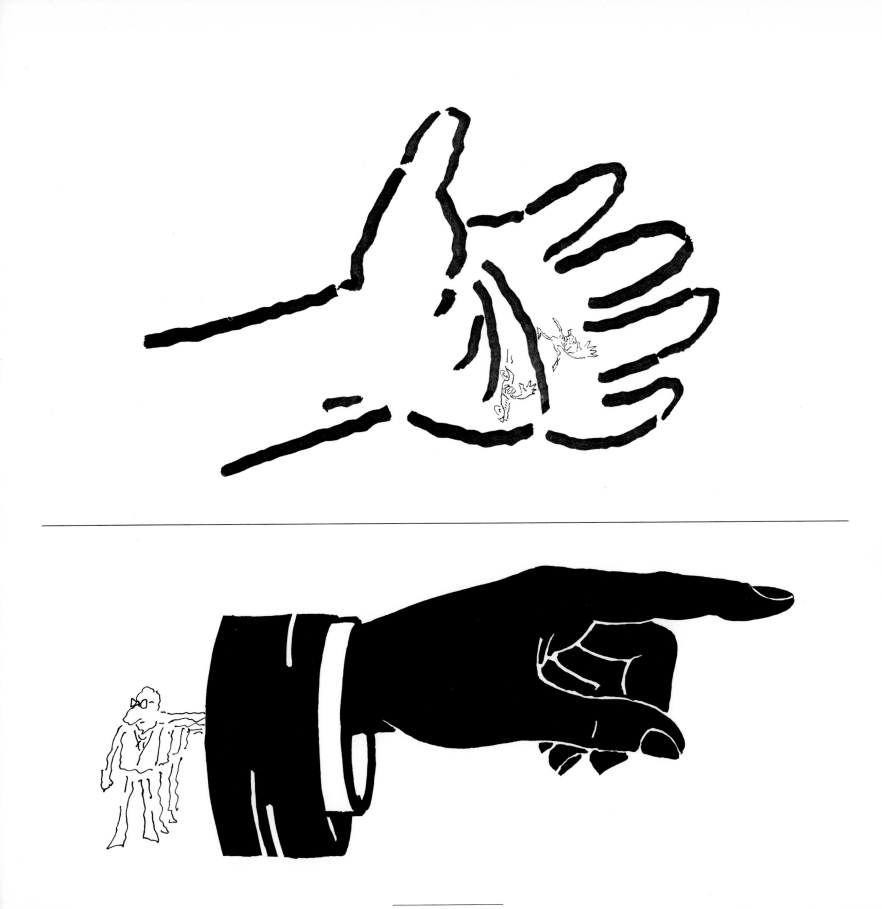

Frames from
"No Room at the Inn," 1978.

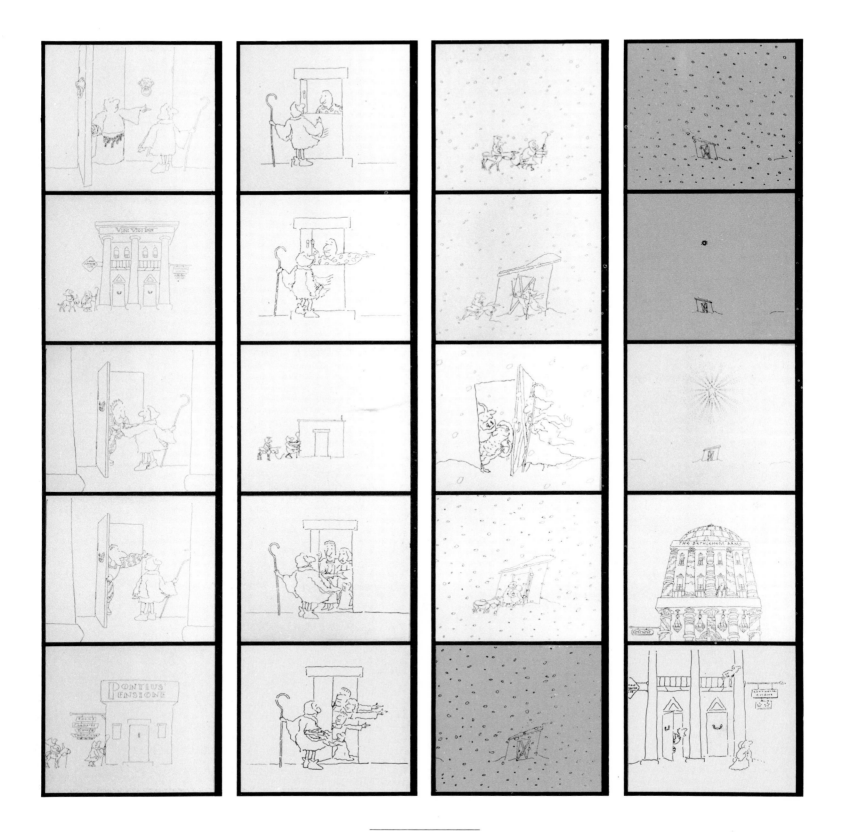

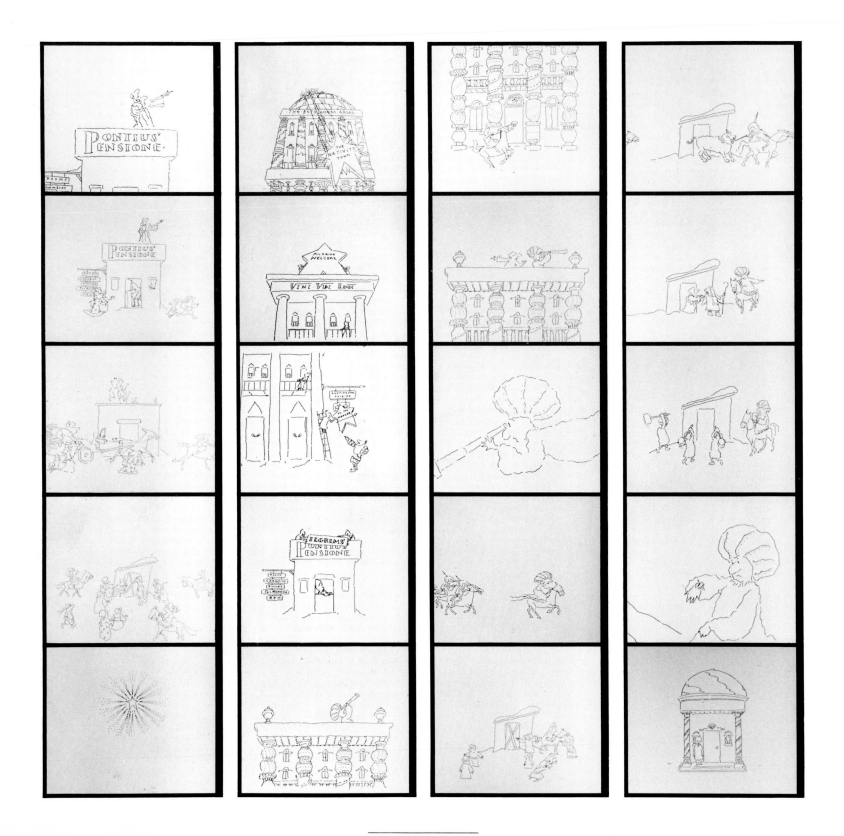

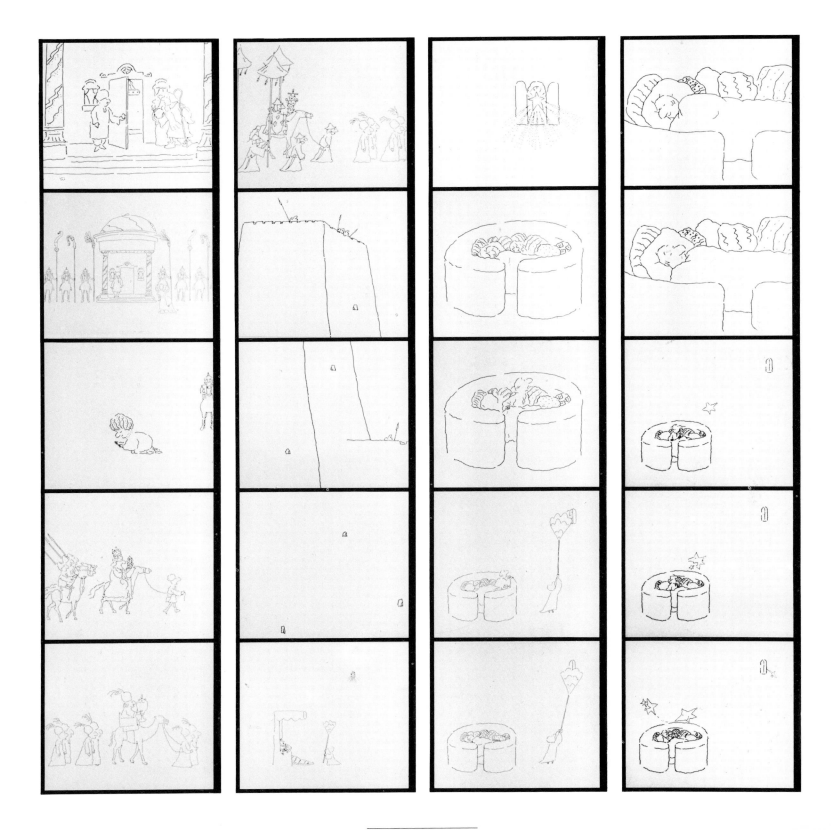

Good luck
go with thee,
farewell.
HENRY V

Adieu, til you return
MACBETH

sweets to the
sweet, Farewell
HAMLET

Go your ways,
and play, go
THE MERRY WIVES
OF WINDSOR

Farewell to you,
and you, and you
JULIUS CAESAR

Last mural
of traveling exhibit
"Shakespeare:
The Globe and the World,"
1979 (8' x 24').

arewell, and thanks!

ANTONY AND CLEOPATRA

Leave me?
Do not go.

A MIDSUMMER
NIGHT'S DREAM

Adieu.

OTHELLO

parting is such
sweet sorrow.

ROMEO AND JULIET

Good Fortune,,,
and farewell,

ANTONY AND CLEOPATRA